THE LAHEY CLINIC GUIDE TO

COOKING
THROUGH
CANCER

THE LAHEY CLINIC GUIDE TO

COOKING
THROUGH
CANCER

100+ Recipes for Treatment and Recovery

LAHEY CLINIC Sophia Gordon Cancer Center

THE COUNTRYMAN PRESS · WOODSTOCK, VT.

CIP DATA ARE AVAILABLE

Cooking Through Cancer

978-1-58157-152-3

INTERIOR PHOTOGRAPHS by Leise Jones Photography

BOOK DESIGN AND COMPOSITION by Michelle Farinella Design

Photographs on pages 39, 48, 67, 79, 108, and 147 by Michele McDonald Photography

Published by The Countryman Press, P.O. Box 748, Woodstock, VT 05091

Distributed by W. W. Norton & Company, Inc., 500 Fifth Avenue, New York, NY 10110

Printed in China

10 9 8 7 6 5 4 3 2 1

This cookbook is dedicated to the patients and families of the
Sophia Gordon Cancer Center at Lahey Clinic—our inspiration.

Preface

WHAT YOU EAT IS IMPORTANT. Your choice of foods, and how you eat them, is a very personal thing: it reflects your tastes and desires, how you feel at different moments, and can even be an expression of your personality. Eating can be a social occasion, an excuse to meet someone, a willful experiment in new sensations, a celebration, or a search for comfort. The food you eat can be fun and different or a safe routine; it can be a political statement, a demonstration of faith, a moral decision, and a mirror for how you feel about yourself and your body.

Eating can be an extravagant experience or a quick fill-up, and it can be different things at different times. It is necessary and always part of your life, but eating should not become a chore or a mere obligation to feed the body. Just as it changes your body and alters your mental outlook, cancer (and its treatment) will transform your meals and give them new meanings.

This book is made up of recipes that we have collected and tested specifically for the many needs of people undergoing cancer therapy. But it is about much more than just getting through the process of having cancer: it is about finding and retaining parts of the life you thought you lost to the disease. The book is about reclaiming something that cancer frequently takes away from people—the enjoyment of food—and using this as a way to assert control over at least this one aspect of your life and health.

Cancer is such a drastic attack on the body, and the prescribed treatment of chemotherapy or hormones or radiation creates such an alien health routine, that people can feel they are no longer in charge of their own medical destiny. Food can sometimes seem unimportant or undesirable during treatment, but it remains necessary. It is nutrition to keep your body going, fuel to continue moving forward, medicine to combat symptoms, and an anchor for retaining normal social activities. Eating is a way to reassert control over some part of what is happening to you.

Food will not cure the cancer or radically change its course, but it can certainly make your treatments easier to weather. Cancer and its treatments can cause loss of appetite, inability to taste, feel, or sometimes even swallow your old favorite foods. It is important to appreciate these changes and acknowledge them by finding new favorites in taste or texture that are more appealing as your treatment progresses. Eating becomes part of your health maintenance: for instance, this book has examples of what to eat specifically for problems such as dry mouth, constipation, diarrhea, oral ulcers, weight loss or excessive weight gain. Our recipes span a range of nutritious basics, comfort foods, family meals, and retooled gourmet dishes.

We have also included meals of celebration, because as bleak as this process can sometimes be, there will always be moments to celebrate—times when something goes right, the disease has let up a bit or even lost ground, the symptoms abate, you "graduate" and finish therapy, and your life becomes your own again. This book is for those times of hope and happiness.

Keith Stuart, MD
Chair, Department of Hematology and Oncology
Sophia Gordon Cancer Center
Lahey Clinic Medical Center

CONTENTS

Key to Recipe Categories

SM   Sore Mouth

C   Constipation

WLP   Weight-Loss Prevention

D   Diarrhea

WGP   Weight-Gain Prevention

N   Neutropenia

N/V   Nausea and Vomiting

Introduction
Cooking Through Cancer:
Recipes for Life During Treatment

There are lots of popular books about cancer out there—what causes it, where it came from, how to avoid it, how to treat it, what it's like to have it, why it's getting worse, why it's getting better—all written to try to explain even a small part of a complex and kaleidoscopic group of diseases we call cancer. This book is not one of those. This book is meant to help in the care of people who, unfortunately and for whatever reason, already have some type of cancer or related illness. They are no longer looking for prevention, and we do not offer any promise of curing or controlling the disease through changes in diet, lifestyle, or beliefs. Our intention is simply to help patients and their families get through a difficult time with some culinary enjoyment and dietary dignity, one meal at a time.

This book has been crafted by clinicians from the Lahey Clinic who are expert in the art and science of caring for patients with cancer. Our goal is to offer good-tasting and fun recipes that are designed with the management of specific symptoms in mind. As patients progress through the various stages of cancer treatment, there are frequently unavoidable side effects and toxicities of both the therapies and the underlying disease. Problems such as loss of appetite (anorexia), nausea, diarrhea, constipation, excessive weight loss or gain, mouth sores (stomatitis), dry mouth (xerostomia), or lowering of the immune system's white blood cells (neutropenia) can all affect a patient's diet. Depending upon the specific symptom, there may be foods that should be avoided and others that might help. The recipes in this book are therefore organized according to these symptoms and side effects in the belief that what you eat and how you eat it makes a difference.

Eating well is more than just nutrition, and we hope that this book emphasizes the social and emotional aspects of diet during the ordeal of cancer treatment. It is not an easy time for anyone, but maintaining some degree of normalcy in daily life always helps with a successful therapeutic plan. We encourage our patients and their families to try to keep up with as much of their daily life as possible, and eating good meals together is certainly an important part of this. So while we present these healthful dishes as suggestions of what to eat when suffering from a specific symptom, they are also not meant for the patient alone. These recipes are meant to be shared by everyone who cares for and supports the person enduring the disease. Preparing and eating these delicious meals together is also therapy, and we need to remember that life continues, despite the diagnosis and the treatments. We hope that the recipes in this book help as you live through this ordeal, and can keep you cooking through cancer.

These recipes are meant to be shared by everyone who cares for and supports the person enduring the disease.

Altered Taste and Smell

Two-thirds to three-quarters of patients undergoing chemotherapy report difficult alterations in both taste and smell. Besides the obvious problem with enjoyment of meals, this can also lead to important health issues, such as depression and insufficient nutrition Patients can also have trouble cooking because they can't tell by taste or smell whether food is done, and that can lead to food-borne illness from eating spoiled or undercooked food. The cells in the nose and mouth that are responsible for the senses of smell (olfaction) and taste (gustation) are usually short-lived, regenerating every 10 to 14 days. Chemotherapy specifically targets any cell in the body that grows rapidly, so alterations in olfactory and gustatory sense are sometimes inevitable after certain drugs. Normal taste and smell usually return by three months following the completion of therapy.

Food will taste better if the mouth is well hydrated, so patients need to drink plenty of fluids and can suck on sour candies to increase saliva production. A metallic taste is common, and can be minimized by using plastic utensils or masked with spices or sweet candies or sauces. Food aversions (learned dislikes) can occur as your brain associates bad taste or nausea with specific foods, and will last longer than the actual problems with taste and smell. Avoiding eating around the time of chemotherapy or radiation will reduce the chance of this happening.

Foods to try

Dairy: all dairy products

Meat and proteins: fish (if not odoriferous), chicken and other poultry, and eggs

Fruits and vegetables: applesauce, cranberry sauce

Desserts: sugar-free hard candies

Other: chilled or frozen food, mildly flavored foods, bland foods, boiled foods, high-protein foods, sugar-free gum

Foods to avoid

Meat and proteins: red meat

Beverages: tea or coffee

Other: any foods that taste bitter or metallic and any foods that have strong smells

Recommendations for Cancer-Related Taste/Smell Alterations

Reduce consumption of foods that taste metallic or bitter, such as red meat, coffee, or tea.

Increase consumption of high-protein, mildly flavored foods, such as chicken, dairy products, eggs, and fish (if not odoriferous).

Chill or freeze food where practical, to help to reduce odors and flavors.

Choose cooking methods that don't produce strong flavors; boiling or braising rather than sautéing, for instance.

Avoid using perfumes or scented cleaning products, particularly around mealtime.

Marinate meats.

Pair sweet foods (applesauce, cranberry sauce, savory sauces) with meat.

Drink more water with food.

Use plastic utensils instead of metallic silverware.

Eat smaller, more frequent meals.

Brush teeth before meals as well as after.

Serve small portions on large plates (trompe l'oeil).

Chew gum or suck on hard candies (sugar-free brands are best) throughout the day. Try sour-tasting lozenges made with ginger or other herbs formulated to decrease nausea.

Use saliva substitutes or lubricants.

Don't smoke.

SORE MOUTH

Besides nausea, a sore mouth is one of the more obvious side effects from treatment that can interfere with eating. Although it is not very common in general, many chemotherapy drugs and local radiation may cause painful mouth irritation and sores. This can prevent people from enjoying their meals, especially if they contain spicy or acidic foods. This is much more common with certain drugs and with more intensive treatments, such as bone marrow transplantation.

Mouth sores are the most visible portion of a larger problem, that of mucositis. The mucosa, or mucosal membrane, is the term for the cells that line the entire gastrointestinal tract, from the mouth down to the rectum. Mucositis refers to a generalized inflammation of this layer of cells, and represents what happens when these cells are damaged by chemotherapy.

Many drugs that are given for cancer are specifically designed to target rapidly dividing and growing cells, since this is what characterizes cancer cells. However, the cells outlined on the gastrointestinal tract are also rapidly dividing. In fact, in the normal person, they generally replace themselves every three days. This is why they are so vulnerable to chemotherapy, since their normal cell division and replacement process is interrupted.

Mucositis has several stages, beginning with cellular DNA damage from chemotherapy or radiation. As these cells begin to die and the surrounding tissues try to protect themselves, chemicals are released by the body to try to deal with the damage. Even before anything is visible in the mouth, pain may occur because of this irritation, involving the local nerves as well. Cells try to regrow, but more around them are dying, and this process is called inflammation. At this stage, sores or ulcerations become visible and more painful as nerve endings are exposed to food products. This is also a dangerous stage, because local bacterial infections will occur without proper mouth care. In general, symptoms of mucositis peak around seven days after treatment. Eventually, normal cells will repopulate the area and everything will heal.

The recipes in this chapter, and many others throughout the book, are designed to be tasty and fun, without containing ingredients that might irritate or further damage the delicate mucosa of the damaged mouth and gastrointestinal tract. It is most important to talk to your doctor or nurse about local oral therapies that may promote oral comfort, and whether or not it might be advisable to take something for pain before you eat. Oral practices to follow include removing dentures; gently cleaning teeth and gums with a soft toothbrush or sponge toothette; and rinsing with a baking soda solution (1 teaspoon baking soda per quart of water) three to four times per day (after meals and before bedtime). It is also crucial to pay attention to good oral hygiene to prevent infection in the mouth. In the meantime, it is important to drink and eat what you can, when you can!

Banana–Peanut Butter Shake

1 cup skim milk

1 banana, peeled and sliced

1 (1 ¼-ounce) packet Carnation classic French vanilla instant breakfast powder

1 tablespoon cocoa powder

1 ½ tablespoons maple syrup

1 tablespoon natural peanut butter

4 ice cubes

SERVES 1

Place all the ingredients in a blender or food processor and process until smooth; serve.

Also helpful for: WLP, N/V, N

You can use whole milk or soymilk in place of the skim milk.

Nutritional Values

Calories 630, Total Fat 14g, Sat Fat 3g, Cholesterol 15mg, Sodium 370mg, Carbohydrates 100g, Dietary Fiber 5g, Sugar 77g, Protein 28g, Calcium 80%, Iron 30%, Vitamin C 70%, Vitamin A 60%

Mango-Coconut Smoothie

1 mango

½ cup coconut milk

¼ cup coconut yogurt

½ banana

2 ice cubes

SERVES 1

Place all the ingredients in a blender or food processor and process until smooth; serve.

Also helpful for: WGP, N

Soy yogurt may be used in place of the yogurt. Light coconut milk can be substituted. You can store this smoothie in the refrigerator, covered, for 2 days.

Nutritional Values

Calories 360, Total Fat 3.5g, Sat Fat 1g, Cholesterol 10mg, Sodium 75mg, Carbohydrates 79g, Dietary Fiber 7g, Sugar 64g, Protein 10g, Calcium 30%, Iron 6%, Vitamin C 230%, Vitamin A 80%

Creamy Wheat Cereal with Maple Syrup and Bananas

2 large bananas, peeled

2 cups water

2 cups whole milk

½ teaspoon salt

1 cup farina (Cream of Wheat)

½ cup maple syrup

Ground cinnamon (optional)

SERVES 4

1. Chop enough banana to equal 1 cup. Slice the remaining banana and set aside.

2. Combine the water, milk, and salt in a large saucepan and bring a boil. Gradually whisk in the farina. Continue to whisk constantly until the mixture thickens, about 4 minutes. Stir the maple syrup and chopped banana into the cereal.

3. Divide the cereal into bowls, sprinkle with cinnamon, if using, top with the banana slices, and serve immediately.

Also helpful for: N. N/V

Nutritional Values

Calories 400, Total Fat 5g, Sat Fat 2.5g, Cholesterol 10mg, Sodium 360mg, Carbohydrates 81g, Dietary Fiber 3g, Sugar 38g, Protein 9g, Calcium 45%, Iron 70%, Vitamin C 10%, Vitamin A 4%

Cinnamon French Toast

3 large eggs

6 tablespoons half-and-half or whole milk

1 tablespoon granulated sugar

1 tablespoon ground cinnamon

¼ teaspoon vanilla extract

6 (¾-inch-thick) slices soft-crusted French bread or egg bread

2 tablespoons (1 ounce) unsalted butter

¼ cup confectioners' sugar

Warm maple syrup (optional)

SERVES 6

1. Beat the eggs, half-and-half, granulated sugar, 2 teaspoons of the cinnamon, and the vanilla extract in a bowl until combined. Pour into a 9 x 13-inch baking dish.

2. Add the bread and turn to coat. Cover and refrigerate until the bread absorbs the egg mixture, at least 30 minutes or up to 1 day. Whisk the confectioners' sugar and remaining teaspoon cinnamon together in a small bowl and set aside.

3. Melt the butter in a large, heavy skillet over medium heat. Add the bread and cook until golden and cooked through, about 3 minutes per side. Transfer the toast to individual plates and sift the cinnamon sugar over the top. Serve with maple syrup, if using.

Also helpful for: WLP, N

Nutritional Values

Calories 230, Total Fat 10g, Sat Fat 4.5g, Cholesterol 125mg, Sodium 210mg, Carbohydrates 28g, Dietary Fiber 1g, Sugar 8g, Protein 7g, Calcium 8%, Iron 10%, Vitamin C 0%, Vitamin A 8%

Cold Cucumber-Yogurt Soup with Mint

½ English cucumber

1 cup plain low-fat yogurt

½ cup water

1 tablespoon dried mint

1 garlic clove, crushed

½ teaspoon salt

a few fresh mint leaves for garnish (optional)

SERVES 2

1. Peel the cucumber, halve it lengthwise, and remove the seeds. Slice each piece in half lengthwise, then slice crosswise into ¼-inch-thick pieces.

2. Stir the yogurt and water together in a medium bowl until smooth. Stir in the cucumber, mint, garlic, and salt. Refrigerate at least 1 hour before serving. Garnish with fresh mint leaves and diced cucumber.

Nutritional Values

Calories 70, Total Fat 1.5g, Sat Fat 0.5g, Cholesterol 5mg, Sodium 600mg, Carbohydrates 10g, Dietary Fiber 1g, Sugar 6g, Protein 5g, Calcium 15%, Iron 4%, Vitamin C 4%, Vitamin A 2%

Cremini Mushroom Soup

4 cups water

1 pound cremini mushrooms, trimmed

1 tablespoon extra-virgin olive oil

½ cup finely chopped shallots

4 garlic cloves, minced

3 tablespoons white wine

Salt and pepper

Chopped fresh parsley (optional)

Croutons (optional)

SERVES 6

1. Bring the water to a boil in a large pot, add the mushrooms, reduce the heat, and simmer for 30 minutes.

2. Meanwhile, heat the oil in a medium skillet. Add the shallots and garlic and cook for 2 minutes. Add the wine and season with salt and pepper to taste; cook until the wine has evaporated, about 2 minutes. Add the shallot mixture to the mushrooms and simmer for 45 minutes.

3. Let the soup cool slightly. Working in batches, transfer to a blender or food processor and process until smooth.

4. Return the puréed soup to the pot and heat over low heat until hot, about 10 minutes. Ladle into bowls, sprinkle with parsley and croutons, if using, and serve.

Also helpful for: WGP, D, N

Nutritional Values

Calories 60, Total Fat 2g, Sat Fat 0g, Cholesterol 0mg, Sodium 85mg, Carbohydrates 9g, Dietary Fiber 1g, Sugar 2g, Protein 3g, Calcium 2%, Iron 4%, Vitamin C 8%, Vitamin A 2%

Black Bean Soup

1 pound dried black beans, picked over, soaked overnight, and drained

8 cups water

½ cup olive oil

1 cup chopped onion

1 cup chopped green bell pepper

1 cup chopped celery

6 garlic cloves, minced

4 teaspoons white wine vinegar (optional)

1 ½ teaspoons ground cumin, or to taste

Sweet peppers, sliced (for garnish)

SERVES 12

1. Combine the beans and water in a large pot, bring to a boil, reduce the heat, and simmer until the beans are soft, about 30 minutes.

2. Meanwhile, heat the oil in a large skillet over medium heat. Add the onion, chopped green bell pepper, and celery, and sauté until the vegetables are softened and lightly browned. Add the garlic, vinegar, if using, and cumin and cook, stirring, for 3 minutes. Pour ½ cup of the cooking water from the beans into the vegetables, reduce the heat to low, and simmer for 30 minutes.

3. Add the cooked vegetables to the beans and cook for 30 minutes, adding more water if necessary. Ladle into bowls, garnish with sweet peppers, and serve.

Also helpful for: C. WGP. N

If you prefer a smooth soup, purée it in batches in a blender.

The vinegar adds a nice touch but can be omitted if it's too acidic.

This recipe makes a large amount of soup; leftovers freeze well.

Nutritional Values

Calories 230, Total Fat 10g, Sat Fat 1.5g, Cholesterol 0mg, Sodium 500mg, Carbohydrates 26g, Dietary Fiber 6g, Sugar 2g, Protein 9g, Calcium 6%, Iron 10%, Vitamin C 20%, Vitamin A 2%

Simple Cream of Broccoli Soup

5 ½ cups low sodium chicken broth

½ cup water

2 tablespoons (1 ounce) unsalted butter

1 onion, chopped

1 russet potato, peeled and chopped

3 cups chopped broccoli florets and stems

½ cup heavy cream, light cream,
or half-and-half

Grated nutmeg

Salt and pepper

SERVES 4

1. Combine the broth and water in a medium saucepan and bring to a simmer; keep warm.

2. While the broth mixture heats, melt the butter in a large pot over medium-high heat, add the onion, and cook until tender, about 5 minutes. Add the potato and toss to coat with the butter. Add the hot broth mixture and bring to a simmer. Stir in the broccoli and return to a simmer; cook until the potato and broccoli are tender, approximately 15 minutes.

3. Let the soup cool slightly. Working in batches, transfer to a blender or food processor and process until smooth.

4. Return the soup to the pot, add the cream, and heat over low heat until hot, about 5 minutes. Season with nutmeg, salt, and pepper to taste. Garnish with broccoli and serve.

Also helpful for: WLP, N

Nutritional Values

Calories 130, Total Fat 9g, Sat Fat 5g, Cholesterol 30mg, Sodium 650mg, Carbohydrates 12g, Dietary Fiber 2g, Sugar 1g, Protein 3g, Calcium 4%, Iron 4%, Vitamin C 50%, Vitamin A 20%

Buttered Polenta

5 cups water

1 tablespoon extra-virgin olive oil

1 ¼ teaspoons kosher salt

1 cup (5 ounces) polenta

1 ½ tablespoons unsalted butter

SERVES 4

1. Bring the water, oil, and salt to a boil in a large, heavy pot, then add the polenta in a slow stream, whisking. Reduce the heat to medium and continue to whisk for 2 minutes.

2. Reduce the heat to low and cook, uncovered, at a bare simmer, stirring frequently, 45 minutes. Remove from the heat, stir in the butter until melted, and serve.

Also helpful for: N/V. N

Do not use quick-cooking polenta for this recipe.

Nutritional Values

Calories 200, Total Fat 8g, Sat Fat 3g, Cholesterol 10mg, Sodium 610mg, Carbohydrates 27g, Dietary Fiber 2g, Sugar 0g, Protein 3g, Calcium 2%, Iron 8%, Vitamin C 0%, Vitamin A 2%

Cheese and Spinach Quiche

2 large eggs

1 cup whole milk

1 cup all-purpose flour

1 teaspoon salt

1 teaspoon baking powder

1 pound fresh spinach, stemmed and chopped

8 ounces Monterey Jack cheese, shredded (2 cups)

1 tablespoon unsalted butter, melted

SERVES 8

1. Preheat the oven to 350 degrees. Beat the eggs in a large bowl. Add the milk and whisk to combine. Add the flour, salt, and baking powder, and whisk until blended. Stir in the spinach and cheese.

2. Coat a 9-inch pie pan with the melted butter, then pour the filling mixture into the pan. Bake until the quiche is set, about 35 minutes. Let cool slightly and serve.

Also helpful for: WLP, N

Nutritional Values

Calories 230, Total Fat 12g, Sat Fat 7g, Cholesterol 75mg, Sodium 670mg, Carbohydrates 21g, Dietary Fiber 3g, Sugar 2g, Protein 12g, Calcium 30%, Iron 15%, Vitamin C 15%, Vitamin A 50%

Roasted Red Pepper Meat Loaf

¾ cup quick-cooking oats

½ cup skim milk

1 onion, peeled

2 pounds ground turkey

½ cup finely chopped red bell pepper

2 large eggs, lightly beaten

¼ cup ketchup

2 teaspoons Worcestershire sauce

1 teaspoon salt

¼ teaspoon garlic powder

Pepper

¼ cup tomato sauce

SERVES 8

1. Preheat the oven to 350 degrees. Combine the oats and milk in a large bowl and let sit for 5 minutes. Slice one-quarter of the onion into very thin rings and set aside; finely chop the remaining onion and add to the oat mixture.

2. Add the ground turkey, bell pepper, eggs, ketchup, Worcestershire sauce, salt, garlic powder, and pepper to taste to the oat mixture. Using your hands, mix just until well combined.

3. Transfer the mixture to a 9 x 13-inch baking dish and shape into a loaf about 5 inches wide by 2½ inches high. Pour the tomato sauce over the meat loaf and sprinkle with the sliced onions. Bake until no longer pink inside, about 1 hour.

4. Remove the meat loaf from the oven and let rest for 10 to 15 minutes before slicing (it will not be very firm) and serving.

Also helpful for: N

Instead of topping the meat loaf with the tomato sauce, you can squeeze ketchup over the top before baking.

Nutritional Values

Calories 240, Total Fat 10g, Sat Fat 2.5g, Cholesterol 125mg, Sodium 530mg, Carbohydrates 11g, Dietary Fiber 1g, Sugar 5g, Protein 26g, Calcium 6%, Iron 10%, Vitamin C 25%, Vitamin A 10%

Constipation

Changes in bowel function are a common side effect of cancer treatment. One of these changes may be constipation, which means a decrease in your usual frequency or consistency. Causes of constipation could include a specific chemotherapy, anti-nausea and pain medications, decreased fluid or food intake, and a decrease in physical activity. Many medications cause constipation by slowing down the muscular activity of the large intestine. This makes it more difficult for the stool to flow through normally, on a regular basis. Not only that, but it gives the intestine more time to do its intended function, which is to draw water out of the digested food—making everything harder and drier by the time it comes out.

Modifying your activity level and your food and fluid intake can help you maintain regularity. Adding fiber to your meals can be a positive modification. Check with your doctor to make sure increasing fiber intake is safe for you. If so, try to include a high-fiber food at each meal or snack. Increase any fiber content slowly to prevent too much gas, bloating, or abdominal cramps. (And be aware that certain types of over-the-counter fiber pills can cause more gas than others.) The Recommended Daily Allowance (RDA) for fiber is 25 to 35 grams per day. Fluid needs vary based on each individual's treatment process; however, the average person needs a minimum of 64 ounces (8 cups) per day to maintain hydration. Try warm beverages, such as decaffeinated coffee, herbal tea, or hot water, which can help to stimulate bowel movements.

If changing the way you eat doesn't seem to be helping, you may need to have a conversation with your doctor about stool softeners or laxatives. Sometimes probiotics are helpful for changing symptoms of constipation, bloating, and diarrhea. Be sure to keep your medical team up to date on your symptoms.

Foods to try:

Fruits and vegetables: especially prune juice and dried fruits; when possible, leave skin on fresh fruits

Grains: whole grains and cereals with a minimum of 3 grams of fiber per serving

Other: nuts and seeds, beans and lentils

Foods to avoid:

Dairy: high-fat dairy products

Fruits and vegetables: bananas and applesauce

Grains: refined grain products

Other: any low-fiber foods

Healthy Carrot Muffins

¾ cup all-purpose flour

½ cup whole-wheat flour

⅔ cup packed dark brown sugar

2 tablespoons wheat germ

2 teaspoons ground cinnamon

1 teaspoon baking powder

½ teaspoon baking soda

⅛ teaspoon salt

2 large eggs

⅓ cup vegetable oil

1 tablespoon vanilla extract

4 medium carrots, peeled and grated (about 2 cups)

½ cup canned crushed pineapple, drained

MAKES 12 MUFFINS

1. Preheat the oven to 350 degrees. Line a 12-cup muffin pan with paper liners.

2. Whisk all-purpose flour, whole-wheat flour, sugar, wheat germ, cinnamon, baking powder, baking soda, and salt in a large bowl. In a medium bowl, lightly whisk the eggs, then whisk in the vegetable oil and vanilla.

3. Quickly and lightly fold the wet ingredients into the dry ingredients with a rubber spatula. Stir in the carrots and pineapple just until evenly moist; the batter will be very thick. Divide the batter evenly among the muffin cups. Bake until golden and a toothpick inserted in the centers comes out clean, 20 to 25 minutes. Turn muffins out of the pan and let cool on a rack. Serve warm, with butter, if desired.

Also helpful for: N. WLP

Nutritional Values

Calories 180, Total Fat 7g, Sat Fat 1g, Cholesterol 30mg, Sodium 150mg, Carbohydrates 26g, Dietary Fiber 2g, Sugar 15g, Protein 3g, Calcium 4%, Iron 6%, Vitamin C 4%, Vitamin A 70%

Banana-Flaxseed Wrap

1 (8-inch) whole-wheat tortilla

1 tablespoon natural peanut butter or other nut butter

2 teaspoons jelly, any flavor

1 banana, peeled and sliced

¼ cup dried cranberries or other small dried fruit

1 teaspoon ground flaxseeds

1 teaspoon vegetable oil

SERVES 1

1. Spread the tortilla with the peanut butter and jelly. Layer the banana slices on top and then sprinkle with the dried cranberries and flaxseeds. Roll the tortilla up to enclose the filling.

2. Heat the oil in a medium skillet over medium-low heat. Place the tortilla in the skillet to warm through, 3 to 4 minutes, turning the tortilla over halfway through cooking. Cut into slices and serve.

Also helpful for: WLP, N

Serve with fresh fruit pieces and carrot sticks, some warm soup, and a mug of coffee or tea.

Nutritional Values

Calories 480, Total Fat 12g, Sat Fat 2.5g, Cholesterol 0mg, Sodium 380mg, Carbohydrates 89g, Dietary Fiber 9g, Sugar 48g, Protein 9g, Calcium 0%, Iron 4%, Vitamin C 15%, Vitamin A 2%

Lentil Salad with Feta

1 ½ cups brown lentils, picked over and rinsed

⅓ cup fresh lemon juice

⅓ cup chopped fresh parsley

1 tablespoon chopped fresh oregano

2 teaspoons Dijon mustard

Salt and pepper

⅓ cup extra-virgin olive oil

1 garlic clove, peeled and crushed

4 ounces feta cheese, crumbled (1 cup)

1 cup chopped celery

1 cup chopped seedless cucumber

½ cup finely chopped red onion

SERVES 6

1. Place the lentils in a large saucepan and add enough water to cover by 2 inches. Bring to a boil, then reduce the heat and simmer until just tender, approximately 30 minutes. Drain and transfer to a large bowl to cool.

2. While the lentils cook, whisk together the lemon juice, parsley, oregano, mustard, and salt and pepper to taste in a small bowl. Gradually whisk in the olive oil until combined, add the garlic clove and set aside.

3. Add the feta cheese, celery, cucumber and onion to the cooled lentils and mix until combined. Remove the garlic clove from the dressing; pour the dressing over the lentil mixture, toss to combine, and serve.

Also helpful for: WGP

Nutritional Values

Calories 290, Total Fat 16g, Sat Fat 4g, Cholesterol 10mg, Sodium 240mg, Carbohydrates 24g, Dietary Fiber 9g, Sugar 3g, Protein 13g, Calcium 10%, Iron 20%, Vitamin C 25%, Vitamin A 10%

Three-Bean Salad

5 ounces dried great northern beans, picked over, soaked overnight, and drained

5 ounces dried red kidney beans, picked over, soaked overnight, and drained

5 ounces dried black beans, picked over, soaked overnight, and drained

⅓ cup red wine vinegar

2 scallions, sliced

1 teaspoon chopped fresh parsley

½ teaspoon Dijon mustard

Salt and pepper

⅓ cup extra-virgin olive oil

SERVES 6

1. Bring 1 quart water to boil in each of three small saucepans. Add one type of bean to each pot and cook until tender, 20 to 30 minutes. Drain the beans, combine in a large bowl and let cool slightly, then refrigerate until cold, at least 1 hour.

2. While the beans chill, whisk together the vinegar, scallions, parsley, mustard, and salt and pepper to taste in a small bowl. Slowly whisk in the oil to combine. Pour over the cold beans, toss to coat, and serve. Garnish with sliced scallions.

Also helpful for: WGP

To cut down on prep time, substitute canned beans; use one 15-ounce can of each kind.

Feel free to swap in equal amounts of other bean varieties, including green beans, for the kinds listed in this recipe.

Chopped tomato makes a nice addition.

This salad stores and travels well, making it a great choice for picnics.

Nutritional Values

Calories 370, Total Fat 13g, Sat Fat 2g, Cholesterol 0mg, Sodium 20mg, Carbohydrates 46g, Dietary Fiber 14g, Sugar 1g, Protein 18g, Calcium 15%, Iron 35%, Vitamin C 4%, Vitamin A 2%

Garden Tortellini Salad

1 (20-ounce) bag mixed frozen or dried cheese tortellini

2 red bell peppers, stemmed, seeded, and diced into small cubes

Salt

1 pound broccoli, stems and florets cut into bite-size pieces

1 pound carrots, peeled and cut diagonally ¼ inch thick

3 leeks, white and light green parts only, rinsed thoroughly, dried, and very thinly sliced

½ cup extra-virgin olive oil

½ cup chopped fresh basil

¼ cup fresh lemon juice

¼ cup red wine vinegar

2 tablespoons chopped fresh parsley

1 teaspoon chopped fresh oregano

SERVES 6

1. Cook the tortellini according to the package instructions. Drain thoroughly and place in a large bowl with the bell peppers.

2. Bring 2 quarts water and ½ teaspoon salt to a boil in a large saucepan. Add the broccoli and cook until tender and bright green, 1 to 2 minutes. Remove the broccoli from the water using a strainer, shake to dry, and add to the tortellini. Repeat this process with the carrots and leeks.

3. In a medium bowl, whisk the oil, basil, lemon juice, and vinegar until combined and season with salt to taste. Pour the dressing over the tortellini, add the parsley and oregano, and toss to combine. Serve warm or refrigerate until needed.

Also helpful for: WGP

Nutritional Values

Calories 500, Total Fat 27g, Sat Fat 5g, Cholesterol 35mg, Sodium 780mg, Carbohydrates 55g, Dietary Fiber 9g, Sugar 9g, Protein 12g, Calcium 10%, Iron 35%, Vitamin C 260%, Vitamin A 320%

Tuscan Bean Soup

2 tablespoons olive oil

2 garlic cloves, minced

1 pound escarole, chopped

Salt and pepper

4 cups low-sodium chicken broth

1 (15-ounce) can cannellini beans, drained and rinsed

1 ounce Parmesan cheese, grated (½ cup)

2 tablespoons extra-virgin olive oil

SERVES 6

1. Heat the olive oil in a large saucepan over medium heat. Add the garlic and cook until fragrant, about 15 seconds. Add the escarole and a pinch of salt and cook until the escarole is wilted, about 2 minutes.

2. Add the broth and beans, cover, and simmer until the beans are heated through, about 15 minutes. Add the Parmesan cheese, season with salt and pepper to taste, and serve, drizzling each portion with 1 teaspoon extra-virgin olive oil.

Also helpful for: WGP, SM, N, N/V

For a vegetarian soup, simply replace the chicken broth with low-sodium vegetable broth.

Nutritional Values

Calories 180, Total Fat 11g, Sat Fat 2g, Cholesterol 5mg, Sodium 310mg, Carbohydrates 15g, Dietary Fiber 6g, Sugar 1g, Protein 8g, Calcium 10%, Iron 10%, Vitamin C 8%, Vitamin A 35%

Brown Rice with Dates and Oranges

3 cups cooked brown rice (1 cup uncooked)

16 dates, pitted and chopped

1 (10-ounce) can mandarin oranges, drained

2 scallions, sliced

¼ cup golden raisins

¼ cup minced fresh parsley

¼ cup extra-virgin olive oil

Juice of 1 lemon

¼ teaspoon ground cardamom

¼ teaspoon ground cinnamon

¼ teaspoon ground cumin

Pinch red pepper flakes

Salt

SERVES 4

Stir together all the ingredients, including salt to taste, in a large bowl. Serve at room temperature.

Also helpful for: WGP

Nutritional Values

Calories 440, Total Fat 15g, Sat Fat 2g, Cholesterol 0mg, Sodium 20mg, Carbohydrates 73g, Dietary Fiber 7g, Sugar 35g, Protein 6g, Calcium 6%, Iron 10%, Vitamin C 60%, Vitamin A 30%

Whole-Wheat Pasta and Beans

2 ½ tablespoons extra-virgin olive oil

4 ounces pancetta, finely chopped

4 garlic cloves, minced

2 carrots, peeled and finely chopped

1 medium shallot, chopped

1 bay leaf

1 teaspoon dried thyme

Salt and pepper

1 cup dry white wine

1 (15-ounce) can white beans, drained and rinsed

2 cups chicken broth

1 pound whole-wheat spaghetti

2 ounces Parmesan cheese, grated (1 cup)

⅓ cup finely chopped fresh parsley

SERVES 6

1. Heat 2 tablespoons of the oil in a large, deep skillet over medium heat. Add the pancetta and garlic and cook until lightly browned, 3 to 4 minutes. Add the carrots, shallot, bay leaf, thyme, and salt and pepper to taste and cook until the vegetables are softened, about 5 minutes.

2. Add the wine and cook until it has mostly evaporated. Add the broth and beans and bring to a simmer.

3. Meanwhile, bring 4 quarts water to a boil in a large pot. Add the spaghetti and cook until al dente. Drain, return to the pot, and toss with 1 ½ teaspoons of the oil.

4. Remove the bay leaf and add the bean mixture to the spaghetti; stir to combine. Stir in the Parmesan and season with salt and pepper to taste. Ladle into shallow bowls, sprinkle with parsley, and serve.

Also helpful for: WGP, N

This pasta dish is an excellent source of dietary fiber and Vitamin A. Low-sodium chicken broth can be substituted for the regular chicken broth.

Nutritional Values

Calories 650, Total Fat 24g, Sat Fat 8g, Cholesterol 40mg, Sodium 630mg, Carbohydrates 76g, Dietary Fiber 11g, Sugar 4g, Protein 23g, Calcium 35%, Iron 25%, Vitamin C 10%, Vitamin A 80%

Black Bean Burgers

½ onion, coarsely chopped

1 tablespoon chopped garlic

1 (29-ounce) can black beans,
drained and rinsed

1 large egg

2 tablespoons chopped fresh cilantro

2 teaspoons chopped fresh parsley

⅛ teaspoon cayenne pepper (optional)

½ cup dried bread crumbs

Salt and pepper

6 hamburger buns

SERVES 6

1. Preheat a charcoal or gas grill.

2. Pulse the onion and garlic in a food processor until finely chopped. Add half of the black beans, the egg, cilantro, parsley, and cayenne, if using, and pulse to combine. Transfer the mixture to a bowl; add the remaining black beans and the bread crumbs. Season with salt and pepper to taste and mix until well combined.

3. Divide the mixture into six even portions and form into patties. Grill over medium-low heat for about 12 minutes, flipping the burgers halfway through cooking. Toast the hamburger buns on the grill, place each burger on a bun, and serve with your favorite condiments.

Also helpful for: WGP, N

These burgers taste great topped with sautéed onions and served with Honey-Roasted Sweet Potatoes (page 156).

Cook the burgers indoors in a skillet if you don't feel like firing up the grill.

Uncooked burgers can be frozen.

Nutritional Values

Calories 300, Total Fat 3.5g, Sat Fat 0g, Cholesterol 30mg, Sodium 680mg, Carbohydrates 55g, Dietary Fiber 12g, Sugar 6g, Protein 14g, Calcium 10%, Iron 20%, Vitamin C 2%, Vitamin A 2%

Quinoa and Black-Eyed Peas

1 ⅓ cups water

Salt and pepper

¾ cup quinoa, rinsed well and drained

1 teaspoon olive oil

1 onion, chopped

3 garlic cloves, minced

1 ½ cups vegetable broth

1 teaspoon ground cumin

¼ teaspoon cayenne pepper

2 (15-ounce) cans black-eyed peas, rinsed and drained

1 cup frozen corn kernels

½ cup chopped fresh cilantro

SERVES 10

1. Bring the water and 1½ teaspoons salt to a boil in a medium saucepan. Stir in the quinoa, cover, and reduce the heat to medium-low. Simmer until the quinoa has absorbed the liquid and is tender, about 15 minutes. Set aside, and keep warm.

2. Heat the oil in a medium saucepan over medium heat. Stir in the onion and garlic and cook until lightly browned. Add the quinoa, broth, cumin, cayenne, and salt and pepper to taste. Bring the mixture to a boil. Cover, reduce the heat, and simmer for 5 minutes

3. Stir the black-eyed peas and corn into the quinoa and simmer until heated through, about 5 minutes. Add the cilantro, season with salt and pepper to taste, and serve.

Also helpful for: WGP. N

Nutritional Values

Calories 130, Total Fat 1.5g, Sat Fat g, Cholesterol 0mg, Sodium 460mg, Carbohydrates 25g, Dietary Fiber 4g, Sugar 1g, Protein 7g, Calcium 4%, Iron 10%, Vitamin C 4%, Vitamin A 4%

Ginger-Rhubarb Crunch

Filling

1 pound rhubarb, cut into 1-inch pieces
(4 cups)

1 cup frozen cranberries

½ cup maple syrup

¼ cup whole-wheat pastry flour

1 teaspoon vanilla extract

1 teaspoon grated fresh ginger

Topping

1 cup chopped walnuts

½ cup quick-cooking oats

½ cup whole-wheat pastry flour

⅓ cup packed light brown sugar

4 tablespoons (2 ounces) unsalted butter,
cut into 4 pieces and chilled

SERVES 8

1. To make the Filling: Preheat the oven to 350 degrees. Spray a 9-inch deep-dish pie pan with nonstick cooking spray. Line a baking sheet with aluminum foil.

2. Toss the rhubarb, cranberries, and maple syrup together in a large bowl. Let stand 15 minutes, tossing frequently. Add the flour, vanilla, and ginger to the fruit mixture and stir to combine. Pour the fruit mixture into the prepared pie pan and spread into an even layer. Place the pie pan on the prepared baking sheet and bake until the juices are bubbling and slightly reduced, about 20 minutes.

3. To make the Topping: While the filling bakes, combine the flour, sugar, oatmeal, and nuts in a medium bowl. Cut in the butter with a pastry cutter, a fork, or your fingers until it is incorporated and the butter is pea-sized. Refrigerate until needed.

4. Remove the pan from the oven, sprinkle the topping evenly over the fruit, and bake until the topping is golden brown, 30 to 40 minutes longer. Let cool slightly; serve warm or at room temperature.

Also helpful for: N, N/V

Baking this dessert on a baking sheet avoids a mess from bubbled-over fruit juices.

Nutritional Values

Calories 310, Total Fat 16g, Sat Fat 4.5g, Cholesterol 15mg, Sodium 10mg, Carbohydrates 40g, Dietary Fiber 4g, Sugar 24g, Protein 5g, Calcium 10%, Iron 6%, Vitamin C 10%, Vitamin A 4%

Weight-Loss Prevention
(High-Calorie Recipes)

Many people with cancer experience a loss of appetite and a decrease in food intake, which can result in significant weight loss. Preventing weight loss is important to help your body heal and recover from the side effects of cancer therapy. Chemotherapy and radiation therapy are used to destroy cancer cells, but they may also damage normal cells. Rebuilding normal cells requires a higher caloric intake and stores of good protein. Preventing weight loss can also help to combat muscle wasting, weakness, and fatigue and improve immune function. Maintaining (or, if necessary, gaining) weight during treatment gives your body energy. Successful weight-loss prevention requires that you eat foods that are high in protein and fat. High-protein foods include eggs, cheese, whole milk, fish, meat, poultry, and beans. Adding nonfat dry milk to soups and sauces is a great way to add protein without adding volume and making you feel full. Selecting high-protein, high-calorie snacks like pudding, milk shakes, or fruit smoothies, and meal replacement drinks or bars can make a big difference in preventing weight loss. Adding fat to your diet can be as simple as adding butter or oil to your food; each tablespoon is approximately 100 calories. Peanut butter and mayonnaise are also high in fat and should be used freely. Remember, the time to go on a diet is not while undergoing cancer treatment.

In addition to loss of appetite, taste alteration is one of the most common and vexing experiences of cancer patients. It can lead to loss of well-being and, in some cases, significant weight loss. Food preferences, tastes, and traditions regarding meal preparation are personal. Often when people become ill, they're offered their favorite foods to stimulate appetite and enthusiasm about eating. Unfortunately, this tactic is usually unsuccessful in cancer-associated loss of appetite. The tastes of favorite foods become so altered that repetitive offering of these foods not only discourages eating, but can lead to long-term "conditioning" against them.

Chemotherapy and radiation therapy are well known for altering the way food tastes. These taste changes are unique to the individual experiencing them. Some people may taste food as overly sweet, metallic, or bland. The smell of certain foods may produce nausea or diminish your appetite. Identifying which foods or odors cause you the most trouble is a good first step in managing this symptom. Being flexible and willing to try different foods during this period of altered taste sensations will also help you to maintain your weight.

Unfortunately the cause and remedy of these side effects are not well understood. Normal cells and cancer cells are known to produce substances called cytokines. These substances may contribute to muscle wasting, a feeling of fullness after eating, lack of appetite and/or taste changes. Another theory contends that cancer cells may use the "fuel" derived from food less efficiently, producing $1/16$ of the energy that a normal cell produces. This can contribute to muscle wasting and weight loss. These symptoms are aggravated by certain types of chemotherapy, biotherapy, and radiation therapy.

The following weight-loss prevention strategies are successful:

Try to keep a list of what foods have an altered taste and avoid those foods while on treatment.

Try foods that you never cared for in the past; these could become your new favorites.

Avoid warm meats like steak; instead try cold meat, like a roast beef sandwich.

Avoid the smells of cooking, if possible.

Try new or different foods, like smoked meat or fish, pickled eggs, or different ethnic cuisines.

If food tastes overly sweet, try adding acidic ingredients such as ketchup, hot sauce, relish, or a squeeze of lemon or lime.

If food tastes metallic, try eating with a plastic fork or spoon.

If food has no taste, try adding sauces, condiments, or spices.

Eat small portions, more frequently. Graze throughout the day, instead of eating three large meals.

Stock up on "lunch box" foods, such as fruit cups, yogurt or pudding cups, peanut butter crackers, dried fruits, and chips. The small self-contained portions are convenient and can provide needed calories.

Keep small servings of ice cream, frozen yogurt, and bon-bons in the freezer.

Serve a small portion on a large plate; it looks more appetizing than a large portion and may seem less challenging to finish.

Avocados, potatoes, pasta, and breads provide much-needed fat and calories.

Comfort foods are the best! The foods you eat when you are sick are often the best tolerated: soups, toast, sandwiches, etc.

Many people with taste alteration and loss of appetite find that their appetites are best in the morning and worst between 4 and 8 PM. This is a common occurrence thought to be linked to your body's circadian rhythm and its production of natural steroids. Steroids reduce pain and fever, stimulate appetite, and keep you alert. Rising levels of steroids in the morning awaken you. As the day progresses the body's steroid levels drop, and so does your energy and appetite. This effect is more pronounced in people undergoing cancer therapy. Plan your meals accordingly. Breakfast may be the best time to eat meat and other high-protein food; dinner may not be. But you may be able to add a light snack late in the evening.

Remember, there is a fine line between offering food and forcing a person to eat. Weight loss, taste alterations, and loss of appetite are biological phenomena linked to cancer and its treatment, not linked to willpower and the will to live. Being knowledgeable about how your cancer and treatment affects you and your body will help you maintain your weight, energy, and well-being while you're undergoing treatment. Knowing what's best for you and being able to communicate that successfully empowers both you and your loved ones.

Peanut Butter Breakfast Bars

4 cups sweetened oat cereal flakes with raisins, such as Raisin Bran

¾ cup quick-cooking oats

½ cup all-purpose flour

½ cup dried fruit pieces

2 large eggs, lightly beaten

½ cup honey

½ cup chunky peanut butter

⅓ cup (⅔ stick) unsalted butter, melted

SERVES 16

1. Preheat the oven to 325 degrees. Line a 9-inch square baking pan with foil and lightly spray with nonstick cooking spray. Combine the cereal, oats, flour and dried fruit in a large bowl.

2. In a separate bowl, stir together the eggs, honey, peanut butter, and melted butter. Pour over the cereal mixture and mix well. Transfer to the prepared pan and press firmly into an even layer. Bake until the edges are golden brown, 28 to 30 minutes. Let cool completely and cut into bars. Store in an airtight container.

Also helpful for: C. N/V. N

Nutritional Values

Calories 210, Total Fat 9g, Sat Fat 3.5g, Cholesterol 35mg, Sodium 115mg, Carbohydrates 31g, Dietary Fiber 3g, Sugar 16g, Protein 5g, Calcium 2%, Iron 15%, Vitamin C 0%, Vitamin A 8%

Granola and Yogurt

2 cups old-fashioned oats

½ cup sunflower seeds

⅓ cup pumpkin seeds

¼ cup wheat bran

1 tablespoon nonfat dry milk

1 teaspoon ground cinnamon

½ cup honey

2 tablespoons molasses

¼ cup dried cranberries

½ cup dried fruit pieces

4 cups plain or vanilla yogurt

SERVES 8

1. Preheat the oven to 300 degrees. Line a baking sheet with aluminum foil. Combine the oats, sunflower seeds, pumpkin seeds, bran, dry milk, and cinnamon in a large bowl. In a small bowl, mix together the honey and molasses. Pour the honey mixture over the cereal, stirring and tossing until well coated.

2. Turn the mixture out onto the prepared pan and bake until very light brown, 20 to 25 minutes, stirring once halfway through the baking time. Let cool and toss with the cranberries and dried fruit.

3. Divide the yogurt into bowls, top with the granola, and serve.

Also helpful for: C, N

Nutritional Values

Calories 4120, Total Fat 14g, Sat Fat 4.5g, Cholesterol 15mg, Sodium 120mg, Carbohydrates 61g, Dietary Fiber 6g, Sugar 36g, Protein 13g, Calcium 20%, Iron 15%, Vitamin C 2%, Vitamin A 4%

Scrambled Eggs with Avocado

1 small avocado, peeled, pitted, and diced

1 tablespoon fresh lemon juice

2 large eggs

1 ounce cheddar cheese, shredded (¼ cup)

2 teaspoons whole milk

Salt and pepper

2 tablespoons (1 ounce) unsalted butter

SERVES 2

1. Toss the avocado with the lemon juice and set aside.

2. Whisk together the eggs, cheese, milk, and salt and pepper to taste in a bowl. Melt the butter in a medium nonstick skillet over medium heat. Add the eggs to the pan and cook, stirring, until the eggs are just set. Divide between two plates, top with the avocado, and serve.

Also helpful for: SM, N

Serve with fresh fruit and warm tortillas.

Nutritional Values

Calories 400, Total Fat 35g, Sat Fat 14g, Cholesterol 225mg, Sodium 170mg, Carbohydrates 105g, Dietary Fiber 6g, Sugar 53g, Protein 13g, Calcium 15%, Iron 8%, Vitamin C 20%, Vitamin A 20%

Chicken Salad

1 tablespoon unsalted butter or vegetable oil

½ onion, thinly sliced

1 pound boneless, skinless chicken breasts, trimmed

2 tablespoons mayonnaise

2 tablespoons sour cream

1½ teaspoons chopped fresh tarragon, or ½ teaspoon dried

Salt and pepper

½ cup seedless grapes, sliced

¼ cup chopped celery (optional)

2 tablespoons chopped pecans, almonds, or walnuts (optional)

SERVES 4

1. Melt the butter in a large skillet over medium heat. Arrange the onion slices in a single layer in the pan, then place the chicken breasts on the onion. Cook until the chicken registers 160 degrees, turning the breasts halfway through cooking. Transfer the chicken to a plate and refrigerate until completely cool; discard the onion.

2. While the chicken cools, whisk the mayonnaise and sour cream together in a small bowl, then whisk in the tarragon and salt and pepper to taste. Transfer the chicken to a platter and let cool.

3. When the chicken is cool, cut it into ¼-inch pieces and place in a large bowl. Add chopped tarragon and salt and pepper to taste. Add the dressing and stir to blend. Add the grapes, celery, and pecans, if using, and stir to coat with the dressing. Season with salt and pepper to taste. Chill until ready to serve.

To reduce the saturated fat, substitute low-fat mayonnaise and sour cream for the full-fat versions and use olive oil instead of butter. Serve this salad on bread or a bed of lettuce.

Nutritional Values

Calories 240, Total Fat 13g, Sat Fat 4g, Cholesterol 90mg, Sodium 180mg, Carbohydrates 5g, Dietary Fiber 1g, Sugar 3g, Protein 25g, Calcium 2%, Iron 2%, Vitamin C 10%, Vitamin A 4%

African Peanut Stew

2 tablespoons plus 1 teaspoon peanut oil

1 tablespoon curry powder

1 teaspoon ground cumin

2 onions, sliced (about 4 cups)

2 large sweet potatoes (about 2 pounds), peeled and cut into chunks

2 teaspoon minced garlic

2 cups low-sodium chicken broth

1 (28-ounce) can whole tomatoes, drained and quartered

1 pound turkey, ground

1 teaspoon salt

¼ teaspoon pepper

½ cup peanut butter

½ cup coconut milk

¼ teaspoon cayenne pepper (optional)

SERVES 10

1. Heat 2 tablespoons of the oil in a large pot over medium-high heat. Add the curry powder and cumin and cook, stirring constantly, for 1 minute. Add the onions and sweet potatoes and cook, stirring constantly, for 2 minutes. Add the garlic and cook for 1 minute. Stir in the broth and tomatoes and bring the soup to a boil. Reduce the heat, cover, and simmer for 20 to 30 minutes.

2. Meanwhile, heat the remaining 1 teaspoon oil in a large skillet. Add the turkey, salt, and pepper and cook, stirring with a wooden spoon to break up any clumps, until cooked through. Transfer to a paper towel–lined plate to drain.

3. Add the turkey, peanut butter, coconut milk, and cayenne, if using, to the soup and stir to combine. Simmer for 20 minutes, then serve. Garnish with parsley if desired.

Also helpful for: N

Cooked, shredded chicken meat may be substituted for the turkey; skip step 2 and add the chicken with salt and pepper to taste in step 3.

You can make this soup vegetarian by substituting an equal amount of vegetable broth for the chicken broth, omitting the turkey, and adding two 15-ounce cans chickpeas (drained) in step 3.

Nutritional Values

Calories 390, Total Fat 20g, Sat Fat 6g, Cholesterol 40mg, Sodium 630mg, Carbohydrates 35g, Dietary Fiber 7g, Sugar 10g, Protein 19g, Calcium 8%, Iron 15%, Vitamin C 30%, Vitamin A 330%

Curried Butternut Squash Soup

1 tablespoon peanut oil

1 small (1 ½ - to 2-pound) butternut squash, peeled, seeded, and cut into 1-inch chunks

1 cup chopped onion

3 garlic cloves, minced

Grated zest and juice of 1 lime

¼ teaspoon ground turmeric

½ cup water

1 teaspoon Thai red chili sauce

4 cups vegetable broth

1 tablespoon grated fresh ginger

16 ounces soft tofu, drained well and cut into 1-inch pieces

1 (14-ounce) can coconut milk

10 tablespoons carrot juice

¼ cup chopped fresh cilantro leaves

2 tablespoons coarsely chopped fresh basil

½ cup plain yogurt

SERVES 6

1. Heat the oil in a large pot over medium heat, add the squash, onion, garlic, lime zest, and turmeric, and cook for 5 minutes, stirring often. Add the water and chili sauce and stir to incorporate, then add the broth. Bring the mixture to a boil, reduce the heat to low, cover the pot, and simmer until the squash is tender, about 20 minutes. Add the tofu.

2. Working in batches, transfer the soup to a blender or food processor and process until smooth.

3. Return the puréed soup to the pot, add the coconut milk, carrot juice, lime juice, cilantro, and basil, and heat over low heat until hot, about 10 minutes. Divide into bowls, top with a dollop of yogurt, and serve.

Also helpful for: N

Nutritional Values

Calories 370, Total Fat 24g, Sat Fat 16g, Cholesterol 5mg, Sodium 210mg, Carbohydrates 29g, Dietary Fiber 6g, Sugar 8g, Protein 12g, Calcium 30%, Iron 35%, Vitamin C 60%, Vitamin A 370%

Coconut Curry Lentil Stew

4 ½ cups water, plus extra as needed

2 tablespoons canola oil

1 small onion, chopped

6 garlic cloves, minced

5 large tomatoes, cored and chopped

1 (14-ounce) can coconut milk

3 tablespoons curry powder

1 tablespoon molasses

⅛ teaspoon ground cinnamon

⅛ teaspoon ground coriander

2 cups red lentils

½ cup chopped fresh cilantro, plus extra for garnish

Salt and pepper

2 cups quinoa, rinsed well and drained

SERVES 12

1. Heat the oil in a large saucepan over medium heat. Add the onion and garlic; cook, stirring, until the onion has softened and turned translucent, about 5 minutes. Stir in the tomatoes and cook for 5 minutes. Add 1 cup of the water, the coconut milk, curry powder, molasses, cinnamon, and ground coriander. Stir to combine, bring to a simmer over medium-high heat, then add the lentils and cook until just tender, about 25 minutes, stirring frequently and adding additional water if needed. Add the cilantro and salt and pepper to taste.

2. While the lentils are cooking, bring the remaining 3 ½ cups water and 1 teaspoon salt to a boil in a medium saucepan. Stir in the quinoa, cover, and reduce the heat to medium-low. Simmer until the quinoa has absorbed the liquid and is tender, about 15 minutes.

3. Spoon the quinoa onto individual plates and ladle the lentil stew over the quinoa. Sprinkle with cilantro and serve.

Also helpful for: N. C

Nutritional Values

Calories 330, Total Fat 12g, Sat Fat 6g, Cholesterol 0mg, Sodium 220mg, Carbohydrates 45g, Dietary Fiber 8g, Sugar 4g, Protein 14g, Calcium 6%, Iron 30%, Vitamin C 20%, Vitamin A 15%

Stuffed Baked Potatoes

4 large baking potatoes

1 tablespoon unsalted butter

½ cup chopped onion

3 ounces ham, chopped (½ cup)

½ cup chopped roasted red pepper

½ cup sour cream

Salt and pepper

2 ounces cheddar cheese, shredded (½ cup)

SERVES 8

1. Preheat the oven to 400 degrees. Scrub the potatoes and pierce with a knife. Bake until the potatoes are tender when pierced with a fork, about 1 hour. Let cool slightly. Leave the oven on.

2. While the potatoes are baking, melt the butter in a medium skillet over medium heat. Add the onion and cook until translucent. Add the ham and roasted pepper and cook briefly to heat through.

3. Cut the baked potatoes in half. Scoop out the potato pulp with a spoon, leaving the sides about ¼ inch thick. Combine the potato pulp, onion-ham mixture, and sour cream, and season with salt and pepper to taste. Spoon the mixture back into the potato shells and top with the cheddar cheese. Bake until the cheese is melted, about 5 minutes, and serve.

Also helpful for: SM, N, N/V

Nutritional Values

Calories 320, Total Fat 16g, Sat Fat 10g, Cholesterol 50mg, Sodium 340mg, Carbohydrates 35g, Dietary Fiber 4g, Sugar 3g, Protein 11g, Calcium 15%, Iron 8%, Vitamin C 70%, Vitamin A 15%

Macaroni and Cheese

1 pound rotini

½ cup (4 ounces) unsalted butter

1 cup panko bread crumbs

½ cup all-purpose flour

5 ½ cups 2 percent low-fat milk

18 ounces cheddar cheese, shredded
(4½ cups)

8 ounces Gruyère cheese, shredded (2 cups)

2 teaspoons salt

¼ teaspoon grated nutmeg

¼ teaspoon pepper

¼ teaspoon cayenne pepper, or to taste

SERVES 12

1. Preheat the oven to 375 degrees. Butter a
   3-quart casserole dish or a 9 x 13-inch baking
   dish and set aside.

2. Bring 4 quarts water to a boil in a large pot.
   Add the rotini and cook until almost al dente
   (tender outside but firm inside). Transfer the
   pasta to a colander, rinse under cold running
   water, and drain well.

3. While the pasta is cooking, melt the butter
   in a large saucepan over medium heat. Stir 2
   tablespoons of the butter into the panko and set
   aside. Add the flour to the remaining butter and
   cook, whisking, for 1 minute. Slowly pour in
   the milk, whisking constantly, and cook until
   the mixture bubbles and becomes thick. Off the
   heat, stir in 3 cups of the cheddar, 1 ½ cups
   of the Gruyère, the salt, nutmeg, pepper,
   and cayenne.

4. Add the cooked pasta to the cheese sauce, then
   pour the mixture into the prepared dish.
   Sprinkle the remaining 1 ½ cups cheddar,
   remaining ½ cup Gruyère, and the bread
   crumbs over the top and bake until browned,
   about 30 minutes. Let cool for 5 minutes
   and serve.

Also helpful for: SM, N

Nutritional Values

Calories 550, Total Fat 30g, Sat Fat
19g, Cholesterol 95mg, Sodium 780mg,
Carbohydrates 43g, Dietary Fiber 2g, Sugar
7g, Protein 26g, Calcium 60%, Iron 10%,
Vitamin C 0%, Vitamin A 20%

Orzo with Zucchini Pesto

4 medium zucchini, diced

Salt and pepper

1 pound orzo

2 cups packed fresh basil leaves,
plus basil sprigs for garnish

½ cup olive oil

1 garlic clove, peeled

SERVES 6

1. Place the zucchini in a large colander, sprinkle
   with 1 tablespoon salt, and toss lightly. Let
   the zucchini drain for 30 minutes, stirring or
   shaking twice. Squeeze the zucchini dry in a
   kitchen towel.

2. Meanwhile, bring 4 quarts water to a boil in a
   large saucepan. Add the orzo and cook until
   just tender, stirring occasionally, 10 to 15
   minutes. Drain the pasta, add to the zucchini,
   and let cool to room temperature.

3. While the pasta cools, process the basil leaves
   and oil in a food processor for 1 minute,
   stopping to scrape down the sides of the bowl.
   With the processor running, add the garlic and
   process until smooth. Add the pesto to the
   zucchini and pasta and season with salt and
   pepper to taste. Garnish with basil sprigs
   and serve.

Also helpful for: SM

Nutritional Values

Calories 470, Total Fat 22g, Sat Fat
4g, Cholesterol 5mg, Sodium 1240mg,
Carbohydrates 57g, Dietary Fiber 3g, Sugar
3g, Protein 12g, Calcium 10%, Iron 15%,
Vitamin C 8%, Vitamin A 15%

Apple Kuchen

1 cup all-purpose flour

1 cup whole-wheat flour

⅔ cup plus ¼ cup packed brown sugar

½ teaspoon salt

⅔ cup (1 ⅓ sticks) unsalted butter, cut into 10 pieces and chilled

4 McIntosh apples, peeled, cored, and sliced

2 large eggs, lightly beaten

1 cup sour cream

½ teaspoon ground cinnamon

½ teaspoon grated nutmeg

SERVES 4

1. Preheat the oven to 375 degrees. Grease a 9 x 13-inch baking pan. Whisk the all-purpose flour, whole-wheat flour, 2/3 cup of the brown sugar, and the salt together in a medium bowl. Using a pastry cutter or your fingers, cut the butter into the dry ingredients until incorporated; the mixture will have a sandy texture.

2. Pour the mixture into the prepared pan and press into an even layer. Arrange the sliced apples over the crust mixture and sprinkle with 2 tablespoons of the brown sugar. Bake until the apples are soft, about 15 minutes. Meanwhile, whisk the eggs, sour cream, cinnamon and nutmeg in a medium bowl to combine.

3. Remove the pan from the oven and pour the sour cream mixture evenly over the apples. Sprinkle with the remaining 2 tablespoons brown sugar and bake until browned and bubbling, 30 minutes. Serve warm or at room temperature.

Also helpful for: SM. N. N/V

Nutritional Values

Calories 840, Total Fat 44g, Sat Fat 26g, Cholesterol 200mg, Sodium 410mg, Carbohydrates 105g, Dietary Fiber 6g, Sugar 53g, Protein 13g, Calcium 10%, Iron 20%, Vitamin C 10%, Vitamin A 30%

Cookies and Cream Pudding

1 (3.4-ounce) package vanilla instant pudding

½ cup dry milk powder

1 cup whole milk

1 cup heavy cream

8 chocolate sandwich cookies,
such as Oreos, crushed

SERVES 4

1. Whisk together the pudding mix and dry milk powder in a medium bowl. Whisk in the milk and cream and continue to whisk for 2 minutes.

2. Layer the pudding and crushed cookies in small bowls or parfait glasses. Let sit until soft-set, about 5 minutes, before serving, or refrigerate until needed.

Also helpful for: SM, N

Instead of layering the cookies and pudding, you can simply stir them together and divide the mixture among the four bowls.

Nutritional Values

Calories 520, Total Fat 33g, Sat Fat 19g, Cholesterol 105mg, Sodium 380mg, Carbohydrates 49g, Dietary Fiber 1g, Sugar 37g, Protein 8g, Calcium 25%, Iron 6%, Vitamin C 2%, Vitamin A 25%

Bread and Butter Pudding

½ loaf French-type bread, such as a baguette, cut into 3/4-inch cubes (about 4 cups)

2 tablespoons (1 ounce) unsalted butter, melted

¾ cup 1 percent low-fat milk

¾ cup heavy cream

2 large eggs

⅓ cup sugar

½ teaspoon vanilla

Pinch salt

2 peaches, peeled, pitted, and sliced

SERVES 4

1. Preheat the oven to 350 degrees. Place the bread in an 8-inch square baking pan, drizzle with the butter, and toss to coat all the cubes.

2. Whisk together the milk, cream, eggs, sugar, vanilla, and salt and pour over the bread, stirring to coat. Cover with plastic wrap and refrigerate for 1 hour.

3. Unwrap the pudding, top with the peach slices, and bake until the pudding is just set but still trembles slightly, about 50 minutes. Serve warm or at room temperature.

Also helpful for: SM, N

You can store the unbaked pudding, wrapped, overnight in the refrigerator.

Nutritional Values

Calories 410, Total Fat 25g, Sat Fat 15g, Cholesterol 170mg, Sodium 170mg, Carbohydrates 38g, Dietary Fiber 1g, Sugar 27g, Protein 8g, Calcium 10%, Iron 4%, Vitamin C 10%, Vitamin A 25%

DIARRHEA

Diarrhea can be caused by many factors during cancer treatment, including chemotherapy, radiation therapy, infection, medications, or food sensitivity. Damage to the intestines can cause digested food to move too quickly through them (decreased transit time), so there is not enough time for the excess fluid to be absorbed. Other possible causes include damage that leads to increased production of fluid from the intestines, or that interferes with the normal ability of the bowel lining to absorb liquids. It's important to first understand the cause of the diarrhea in order to best manage the symptom, so be sure to consult your doctor. Often there is more than one inciting event.

Diarrhea can lead to dehydration, which means that your body doesn't have enough fluids to work properly. For severe diarrhea, intravenous fluids are often required. Occasionally patients require hospitalization to maintain adequate hydration.

Signs of dehydration include:

Dizziness or lightheadedness, especially when changing positions or first standing up

Dry mouth or dry skin

Constant thirst

Loss of appetite

Fatigue and weakness

Dark colored urine or decreased urine output

Fevers or chills

Palpitations (rapid heart rate)

When dehydration is more severe, it can cause:

Muscle cramps

Headaches

Tingling of the limbs

Painful urination

Confusion

Difficulty breathing

Seizures

Unconsciousness

If you have diarrhea, to prevent dehydration you should drink plenty of fluids, preferably at room temperature. Be aware that not all fluids are beneficial; some contain simple sugars, which may worsen the diarrhea by osmotic effects (this means that the high concentration, or density of the molecules, actually draws liquid out of the intestinal wall and leads to watery stools). Beverages that fall into this category include soft drinks and undiluted apple juice (foods like sweetened cereals should be also avoided for this reason). The best fluids to drink are those that replace electrolytes in your system, such as fat-free broth, consommé, and fruit juice (cranberry, grape, and fruit blends are good choices). You can also eat Popsicles and gelatin desserts. Finally, instead of three large meals a day, eat several small meals (it's easier on your digestive system), and limit your intake of dietary fiber to about 10 grams per day.

Foods to try:

Meats and proteins: low-fat meats like skinless chicken, turkey, or fish; tofu; hard-cooked or scrambled eggs (though be careful to avoid cooking fats)

Fruits and vegetables: potatoes, applesauce, cooked carrots

Grains: white rice, noodles, Cream of Wheat, white bread

Foods to avoid:

Dairy: all dairy products

Fruits and vegetables: high-fiber vegetables such as corn, beans, peas, cabbage, and cauliflower

Grains: whole grains and whole-grain products such as brown rice, cracked wheat, tabouli, whole-wheat bread or pasta, cornbread, and any bread with dried fruits or nuts

Other: all sources of caffeine, including soda and chocolate; foods high in simple sugars, such as apple juice and sweetened breakfast cereal

Dairy-Free Banana Bread

1 ¼ cups all-purpose flour

1 teaspoon baking soda

¼ teaspoon pumpkin pie spice

1 cup sugar

2 large eggs

3 tablespoons vegetable oil

2 ripe bananas, peeled and lightly mashed

½ cup unsweetened applesauce

1 teaspoon vanilla extract

SERVES 10

1. Preheat the oven to 350 degrees. Grease and flour a 9 x 5-inch loaf pan. Whisk together the flour, baking soda and pumpkin pie spice.

2. In a large bowl, whisk the sugar, eggs, and oil until creamy. Add the bananas, applesauce, and vanilla and whisk until thoroughly combined. Add the flour mixture to the egg mixture and stir until no dry streaks of flour remain.

3. Scrape the batter into the prepared loaf pan. Bake until the top is firm to the touch, the loaf pulls away from the sides of the pan, and a cake tester inserted in the center comes out clean, about 50 minutes. Let the loaf cool completely in the pan on a wire rack.

Also helpful for: SM, WLP, N, N/V

This banana bread will keep, wrapped in plastic wrap and refrigerated, for up to five days.

Nutritional Values

Calories 200, Total Fat 5g, Sat Fat 0.5g, Cholesterol 35mg, Sodium 140mg, Carbohydrates 36g, Dietary Fiber 2g, Sugar 25g, Protein 3g, Calcium 2%, Iron 2%, Vitamin C 4%, Vitamin A 2%

Pumpkin Muffins

1 ½ cups raisins

4 ¾ cups all-purpose flour

4 cups sugar

1 ½ teaspoons baking powder

1 ½ teaspoons baking soda

1 ½ teaspoons salt

1 ½ teaspoons grated nutmeg

1 ½ teaspoons ground cinnamon

1 ½ teaspoons ground cloves

1 (29-ounce) can pumpkin purée

6 large eggs

1 cup unsweetened applesauce

1 cup walnuts, chopped

MAKES 36 MUFFINS

1. Preheat the oven to 350 degrees. Grease three 12-cup muffin tins or line them with paper liners. Cover the raisins with hot tap water and let soak for 10 minutes to plump; drain.

2. While the raisins soak, mix the flour, sugar, baking powder, baking soda, salt, nutmeg, cinnamon, and cloves in a large bowl. In a separate bowl, whisk the pumpkin purée, eggs, and applesauce until smooth. Add this mixture to the dry ingredients and stir thoroughly to make a smooth batter. Stir the raisins and walnuts into the batter.

3. Spoon the batter into the prepared muffin cups. Bake until a toothpick inserted into the center comes out clean, 30 to 35 minutes. Let the muffins cool in the tins for 5 minutes, then turn them out onto a wire rack to cool completely.

Also helpful for: WGP. N. N/V

Wrapped in plastic wrap and placed in a zipper-lock freezer bag, these muffins freeze well. Thaw them by microwaving for 20 to 30 seconds.

Nutritional Values

Calories 230, Total Fat 3g, Sat Fat 0g, Cholesterol 30mg, Sodium 230mg, Carbohydrates 48g, Dietary Fiber 3g, Sugar 28g, Protein 4g, Calcium 2%, Iron 8%, Vitamin C 2%, Vitamin A 40%

Rice Flour Pancakes

1 cup rice flour

1 tablespoon sugar

2 teaspoons baking powder

½ teaspoon salt

1 cup rice milk

1 large egg, lightly beaten

2 teaspoons vegetable oil, plus extra for the pan

Maple syrup, warmed

MAKES 12 PANCAKES; SERVES 4

1. Whisk the rice flour, sugar, baking powder and salt together in a bowl. Beat in the rice milk until the mixture has a smooth consistency. Add the beaten egg and oil and mix until just blended.

2. Heat a large nonstick skillet over medium heat, or heat a nonstick electric griddle to 375 degrees. (The skillet is ready when drops of water splashed on the surface bounce and sizzle.) Lightly oil the pan. Using a scant 3 tablespoons batter per pancake, ladle the batter onto the griddle to form 4-inch cakes. Cook until the bottoms are browned and bubbles appear on the surface. Flip the pancakes over and continue to cook about 2 minutes. Repeat with the remaining batter and serve with warmed maple syrup, if desired.

Also helpful for: SM, N, N/V

Nutritional Values

Calories 390, Total Fat 4g, Sat Fat 0.5g, Cholesterol 45mg, Sodium 620mg, Carbohydrates 86g, Dietary Fiber 1g, Sugar 55g, Protein 3g, Calcium 15%, Iron 2%, Vitamin C 0%, Vitamin A 2%

Cinnamon Coffee Cake

Brown sugar topping

½ cup packed brown sugar

2 teaspoons ground cinnamon

1 tablespoon unsalted butter, melted

Coffee cake

1 cup all-purpose flour

2 teaspoons baking powder

¼ teaspoon salt

½ cup (4 ounces) unsalted butter, softened

1 cup granulated sugar

2 large eggs

1 teaspoon vanilla extract

1 cup plain yogurt

Confectioners' sugar

SERVES 8

1. To make the Brown sugar topping: Preheat the oven to 350 degrees. Spray a 12-cup tube or Bundt pan with nonstick cooking spray. Combine the brown sugar and cinnamon in a small bowl; drizzle in the melted butter and stir with a fork; set aside.

2. To make the Coffee cake: Sift together the flour, baking powder, and salt. With an electric mixer, cream the butter and granulated sugar in a large bowl until light and fluffy. Add the eggs, one at a time, then the vanilla, and mix thoroughly. Add the flour mixture in three batches alternately with the yogurt in two batches, beating after each addition.

3. Pour the batter into the prepared pan. Sprinkle the brown sugar topping on the surface of the batter. Run a knife through the batter in a zig-zag pattern to slightly incorporate the brown sugar mixture. Bake until the edges are golden brown and a cake tester inserted into the center comes out clean, 35 to 40 minutes. Let cool in the pan for 10 minutes before inverting onto a wire rack. Place on a serving platter, dust with confectioners' sugar, and serve warm.

Also helpful for: SM. WLP. N. N/V

Nutritional Values

Calories 360, Total Fat 14g, Sat Fat 9g, Cholesterol 80mg, Sodium 250mg, Carbohydrates 54g, Dietary Fiber 1g, Sugar 40g, Protein 5g, Calcium 10%, Iron 6%, Vitamin C 0%, Vitamin A 10%

Eggs in a Hole

2 teaspoons unsalted butter, softened

4 slices bread

4 large eggs

Salt and pepper

Cheese (optional)

SERVES 4

1. Heat a large skillet over medium-high heat. Butter the bread slices on one side. Using a 2-inch round biscuit cutter, cut a hole in the center of each bread slice.

2. Arrange the bread buttered side down in the skillet. Crack an egg into each hole and cook until the bread is light brown on the bottom and the eggs have begun to set. Using a wide spatula, turn the bread and eggs over and continue to cook until the eggs are done to your liking. Season with salt and pepper to taste and serve.

Also helpful for: SM, WLP

After turning the eggs over in step 2, top each one with cheese if desired, to add calories.

Nutritional Values

Calories 210, Total Fat 7g, Sat Fat 2.5g, Cholesterol 185mg, Sodium 210mg, Carbohydrates 27g, Dietary Fiber 7g, Sugar 5g, Protein 10g, Calcium 6%, Iron 10%, Vitamin C 0%, Vitamin A 6%

Sesame Chicken Noodles

1 pound angel hair pasta

¾ cup low-sodium soy sauce

2 ½ tablespoons toasted sesame oil

2 tablespoons sesame seeds

2 teaspoons ground coriander

½ cup rice wine vinegar

8 ounces cooked chicken breast, shredded

½ cup walnuts, coarsely chopped

1 bunch scallions, sliced

SERVES 8

1. Bring 4 quarts water to a boil in a large pot, add the pasta, and cook until al dente. Drain the pasta and rinse briefly in cold water to cool. Place in a large bowl.

2. While the pasta cooks, whisk together the soy sauce, sesame oil, sesame seeds, and coriander, then whisk in the vinegar.

3. Add the chicken, walnuts, and scallions to the pasta, pour the dressing over the top, and toss to combine. Refrigerate until ready to serve. Garnish with scallions and extra chicken slices upon serving, if desired.

Also helpful for: N/V

Nutritional Values

Calories 340, Total Fat 11g, Sat Fat 1.5g, Cholesterol 10mg, Sodium 890mg, Carbohydrates 45g, Dietary Fiber 3g, Sugar 3g, Protein 13g, Calcium 4%, Iron 15%, Vitamin C 6%, Vitamin A 4%

Italian Turnip Soup with Rice

3 tablespoons (1½ ounces) unsalted butter

3 tablespoons olive oil

1 pound turnips, peeled, and cut into
½-inch pieces

6 cups low-sodium chicken broth

1 cup converted long-grain rice

2 tablespoons minced fresh parsley

Salt and pepper

SERVES 6

1. Melt the butter with the olive oil in a large
   saucepan over high heat. When the foam
   subsides, add the turnips and sauté, tossing
   frequently, until golden brown, 5 to 7 minutes
   Add the broth, bring to a boil, cover, reduce
   the heat to medium, and cook for 10 minutes.

2. Stir in the rice and cook the mixture, covered,
   until the rice is al dente, about 15 minutes. Stir
   in the parsley, season with salt and pepper to
   taste, and serve.

Also helpful for: SM. N. N/V

Nutritional Values

Calories 250, Total Fat 13g, Sat Fat
4.5g, Cholesterol 15mg, Sodium 120mg,
Carbohydrates 29g, Dietary Fiber 1g, Sugar
3g, Protein 5g, Calcium 2%, Iron 10%,
Vitamin C 30%, Vitamin A 6%

Ginger Miso Soup

4 cups vegetable broth

½ cup water

6 shiitake mushrooms, stems removed, sliced

2 teaspoons sugar

1 teaspoon ground ginger

6 ounces tofu, cut into cubes

2 tablespoons white miso

2 ounces rice noodles

½ cup frozen chopped spinach, thawed (optional)

SERVES 4

1. Combine the broth and water in a large saucepan, add the mushrooms, and bring to a boil. Add the sugar and the ginger and cook for 10 minutes.

2. Add the tofu, lower the heat, and simmer. Ladle 1 cup of the liquid from the pot into a small bowl, add the miso, and whisk until smooth. Return the miso mixture to the pot. Add the rice noodles and spinach, if using, and simmer until the noodles are tender, 3 to 4 minutes. Serve.

Also helpful for: SM, WGP, N/V

The mushrooms, tofu, noodles and spinach can be omitted to make a nice clear liquid broth.

Nutritional Values

Calories 150, Total Fat 2.5g, Sat Fat 0g, Cholesterol 0mg, Sodium 890mg, Carbohydrates 26g, Dietary Fiber 1g, Sugar 9g, Protein 6g, Calcium 10%, Iron 8%, Vitamin C 0%, Vitamin A 15%

Brown Rice with Mushrooms

2 tablespoons (1 ounce) unsalted butter

½ onion, chopped

¼ cup chopped cremini mushrooms

1 cup long-grain brown rice

1 ½ cups low-sodium chicken broth

SERVES 6

1. Melt the butter in a medium saucepan over medium heat. Add the onion and mushrooms and cook, stirring, until softened, 5 minutes. Add the rice and continue to cook until the rice is coated and slightly toasted, 1 to 2 minutes.

2. Add the broth and bring to a boil; cover, reduce the heat, and simmer until the rice is tender and all the liquid is absorbed, about 45 minutes. Let the rice sit off the heat for a few minutes, then serve.

Also helpful for: SM. N. N/V

Nutritional Values

Calories 150, Total Fat 4.5g, Sat Fat 2.5g, Cholesterol 10mg, Sodium 20mg, Carbohydrates 23g, Dietary Fiber 1g, Sugar 1g, Protein 3g, Calcium 0%, Iron 0%, Vitamin C 2%, Vitamin A 2%

Light Tomato Pasta

1 pound penne

2 ounces Parmesan cheese

1 pound tomatoes, cored and chopped into ½-inch pieces

2 tablespoons extra-virgin olive oil

1 tablespoon aged balsamic vinegar

1 garlic clove, minced

2 ounces arugula, stemmed

1⅓ cups fresh basil leaves

Salt and pepper

SERVES 6

1. Bring 4 quarts of water to a boil in a large pot, add the penne, and cook until al dente. While the pasta is cooking, grate half of the Parmesan and set aside.

2. Place the tomatoes in a large bowl. Add the oil, vinegar, and garlic and stir. Tear the arugula and basil leaves into small pieces and add to the tomatoes. Using a vegetable peeler, shave the remaining Parmesan into the bowl with the tomato mixture.

3. Add the penne to the tomato mixture and toss to coat. Season with salt and pepper to taste and serve, passing the grated Parmesan at the table.

Also helpful for: WGP

For extra protein, toss chopped cooked chicken with the pasta and sauce.

Nutritional Values

Calories 380, Total Fat 9g, Sat Fat 2g, Cholesterol 5mg, Sodium 135mg, Carbohydrates 59g, Dietary Fiber 3g, Sugar 6g, Protein 14g, Calcium 15%, Iron 10%, Vitamin C 25%, Vitamin A 30%

Baked Haddock

1 teaspoon olive oil

6 (8-ounce) haddock fillets

Salt and pepper

3 tablespoons fresh lemon juice,
plus lemon wedges for serving

½ cup salted cracker crumbs,
such as Ritz (about 12 crackers)

½ cup chopped white mushrooms

¼ cup sliced scallions

2 tablespoons chopped fresh parsley,
plus parsley sprigs for serving

¼ cup water

1 teaspoon unsalted butter, melted

SERVES 6

1. Preheat the oven to 400 degrees. Line a large baking sheet with foil and coat the foil with the olive oil.

2. Arrange the fish on the prepared baking sheet, sprinkle with salt and pepper, and drizzle with 1 tablespoon of the lemon juice. Combine the cracker crumbs, mushrooms, scallions, chopped parsley, and ⅛ teaspoon pepper in a bowl and mix well. Add the water, remaining 2 tablespoons lemon juice, and melted butter and toss to combine. Spoon over the fish fillets and press lightly to help the crumbs adhere.

3. Bake until the fish flakes easily, 30 to 35 minutes, basting every 10 minutes with the pan juices. Remove the fish carefully to a heated serving platter. Top with sprigs of parsley and serve with lemon wedges.

Also helpful for: WGP. N. N/V

Nutritional Values

Calories 240, Total Fat 4g, Sat Fat 1g, Cholesterol 145mg, Sodium 620mg, Carbohydrates 5g, Dietary Fiber 0g, Sugar 1g, Protein 44g, Calcium 4%, Iron 6%, Vitamin C 10%, Vitamin A 6%

Ginger Rice Cakes and Shrimp

1 cup water

½ cup basmati rice

1 tablespoon minced candied ginger

1 teaspoon kosher salt

18 large shrimp, peeled and deveined, tails on if desired

¼ cup extra-virgin olive oil

2 tablespoons fresh lemon juice

Kosher salt and pepper

1 large egg white, lightly beaten

3 tablespoons all-purpose flour

1 teaspoon vegetable oil

2 tablespoons chopped parsley

SERVES 6

1. Bring the water to a boil in a medium saucepan and add the rice, ginger, and 1 teaspoon salt. Stir and return to a boil, then reduce the heat to low, cover, and cook until the rice is tender and the water is absorbed, about 20 minutes. Transfer the rice to a large bowl and let cool until just warm.

2. While the rice cools, preheat a charcoal or gas grill. Toss the shrimp with the oil, lemon juice, and salt and pepper to taste. Let the shrimp marinate for 30 minutes. (Do not overmarinate.)

3. Preheat the oven to 200 degrees. Line a baking sheet with parchment paper and set aside. Add the egg white to the rice and mix well. Add the flour and stir to incorporate. Working with 2 tablespoons at a time, form the rice mixture into a ball, press it flat between your palms, and place on the prepared baking sheet. (You should have 12 rice cakes.)

4. Heat ½ teaspoon of the oil in a large nonstick skillet over medium heat. Add 6 rice cakes and cook until golden brown on both sides, 3 to 4 minutes per side. Transfer to the prepared baking sheet and place in the oven to keep warm. Repeat with the remaining rice cakes.

5. When the rice cakes are nearly done, grill the shrimp until pink, opaque and curled in on themselves, about 2 minutes per side. To serve, place 2 rice cakes on each plate, top with 3 shrimp, and sprinkle with parsley.

Also helpful for: WGP, N

The rice cakes can be made in advance, wrapped, and refrigerated for up to 1 day. To reheat, place them on a parchment paper–lined baking sheet and bake in a preheated 400-degree oven for 5 minutes.

Nutritional Values

Calories 180, Total Fat 10g, Sat Fat 1.5g, Cholesterol 25mg, Sodium 450mg, Carbohydrates 17g, Dietary Fiber 1g, Sugar 1g, Protein 5g, Calcium 2%, Iron 2%, Vitamin C 4%, Vitamin A 2%

Chicken with Rosemary Potatoes

2 tablespoons olive oil

4 pounds bone-in chicken pieces (split breasts cut in half, drumsticks, and/or thighs), trimmed

2 garlic cloves, minced

1 cup white wine

1 cup low-sodium chicken broth

1 tablespoon chopped fresh rosemary

2 pounds white or Yukon Gold potatoes (about 4 potatoes), peeled and cut into ¼-inch pieces

Salt and pepper

SERVES 8

1. Preheat the oven to 350 degrees. Heat the oil in a Dutch oven over medium heat, add half of the chicken pieces and half of the garlic, and cook until the chicken pieces are browned on all sides, 10 to 15 minutes. Transfer the chicken to a platter and repeat with the remaining chicken and garlic.

2. Drain off all but 1 tablespoon of fat and return the chicken to the pot. Add the wine, ½ cup of the broth, and the rosemary, cover, and simmer for 5 minutes. Add the potatoes, season with salt and pepper to taste, and cover.

3. Transfer the pot to the oven and cook until the chicken breasts register 160 degrees, the thighs/drumsticks register 175 degrees, and the potatoes are tender, about 30 minutes, stirring halfway through cooking and adding the remaining ½ cup broth as necessary. Serve.

Also helpful for: WGP, N, N/V

Nutritional Values

Calories 390, Total Fat 13g, Sat Fat 2.5g, Cholesterol 140mg, Sodium 160mg, Carbohydrates 17g, Dietary Fiber 2g, Sugar 2g, Protein 45g, Calcium 4%, Iron 15%, Vitamin C 35%, Vitamin A 2%

Oven-Fried Parmesan Chicken

¾ cup plain nonfat yogurt

¼ cup fresh lemon juice

1 ½ tablespoons Dijon mustard

3 garlic cloves, minced

1½ teaspoons dried oregano

6 boneless, skinless chicken breasts, trimmed

2 cups panko bread crumbs

¼ cup grated Parmesan cheese

1 tablespoon chopped fresh parsley

SERVES 6

1. Whisk together the yogurt, lemon juice, Dijon mustard, garlic, and ½ teaspoon of the oregano in a large bowl. Add the chicken and stir to coat. Cover the bowl with plastic and refrigerate at least 2 hours or overnight.

2. Preheat the oven to 350 degrees. Line a baking sheet with foil and spray with nonstick cooking spray. Combine the panko, Parmesan, parsley, and the remaining 1 teaspoon oregano in a shallow bowl. Drain the chicken in a colander, then dredge each piece in the bread-crumb mixture. Bake until the chicken is tender and golden brown, about 40 minutes. Serve.

Also helpful for: WGP, N, N/V

Nutritional Values

Calories 280, Total Fat 5g, Sat Fat 2g, Cholesterol 85mg, Sodium 360mg, Carbohydrates 24g, Dietary Fiber 1g, Sugar 2g, Protein 30g, Calcium 10%, Iron 4%, Vitamin C 10%, Vitamin A 4%

Mashed Potato-Turkey Patties

1 large egg

1 cup mashed potatoes

4 ounces cooked turkey breast, very finely chopped (about 1 cup)

½ teaspoon dried rosemary

¼ cup all-purpose flour

Salt and pepper

1 teaspoon vegetable oil

MAKES 8 PATTIES

1. Whisk the egg in a medium bowl, add the mashed potatoes, turkey, and rosemary, and stir to combine. In a shallow dish, combine the flour with salt and pepper to taste. Form the turkey mixture into eight 2-inch balls. Lightly dredge the balls in the flour and set on a plate.

2. Heat the oil in a large nonstick skillet over medium heat. Add the balls and flatten into patties with a spatula (they should be about 2 ½ inches wide). Cook until crispy and golden, 10 to 15 minutes, flipping the patties halfway through cooking. Serve.

Also helpful for: SM, D, N

Nutritional Values

Calories 80, Total Fat 2g, Sat Fat 0.5g, Cholesterol 35mg, Sodium 20mg, Carbohydrates 9g, Dietary Fiber 1g, Sugar 0g, Protein 6g, Calcium 2%, Iron 4%, Vitamin C 4%, Vitamin A 0%

Roasted Turkey Breast

1 tablespoon dried rosemary

1 garlic clove, minced

1 teaspoon dried thyme

1 teaspoon dried oregano

½ teaspoon pepper

½ teaspoon paprika

1 (3-pound) turkey breast

1 cup low-sodium chicken broth

SERVES 8

1. Preheat the oven to 375 degrees. Mix together the rosemary, garlic, thyme, oregano, pepper, and paprika.

2. Rinse the turkey breast and pat it dry. Sprinkle the herb mixture evenly over the turkey breast. Place the breast in a shallow baking dish. Add the broth, then add enough water so that the liquid is ¼ inch deep.

3. Roast the turkey breast until it registers 165 degrees. Let rest for 10 minutes, then remove the skin, carve, and serve.

Also helpful for: SM, WGP, N

Serve cold sliced turkey on toast with Dijon mustard.

Dice leftover turkey and add to chicken broth with egg noodles or rice, to make a soup.

Nutritional Values

Calories 270, Total Fat 12g, Sat Fat 3.5g, Cholesterol 110mg, Sodium 110mg, Carbohydrates 1g, Dietary Fiber 0g, Sugar 0g, Protein 38g, Calcium 4%, Iron 15%, Vitamin C 0%, Vitamin A 2%

Weight-Gain Prevention
(Low-Calorie Recipes)

Weight gain during cancer treatment is common. The drugs or the cancer itself can slow down your metabolism, but behavior changes are probably more important. Fatigue makes people less likely to exercise, and they frequently seek out "comfort foods" during treatment, which are usually higher in fat and calories. Knowing what you are going through, friends and family will worry more about your diet than usual and will often encourage you to "have another cookie because you need your strength!"

Nevertheless, you can use a combination of dietary modifications and exercise during and after cancer treatment to help minimize any weight gain generated during treatment and recovery. Maintaining physical activity and practicing portion control are crucial to avoiding unwanted weight gain.

Regular exercise increases your sense of well-being after cancer treatment and can speed your recovery. Cancer patients who exercise often experience

- fewer signs and symptoms of depression

- less anxiety and improved mood

- reduced fatigue

- more restful sleep, and

- stronger immune systems.

Emerging evidence suggests that exercise also reduces the risk of a cancer recurrence or of a cancer-related death. It's unknown whether exercise during cancer treatment has any effect on the treatment's efficacy. No studies have examined this potential interaction. Check with your doctor before you begin any exercise program.

If you exercised regularly before diagnosis, the goal should be to maintain this level as much as possible. If you were sedentary before diagnosis, low-intensity activities such as stretching and short, slow walks should be the first steps. Increase any activity slowly. Take the stairs more often or park farther from your destination and walk the rest of the way. Focus on strength-building exercises if you have lost muscle or gained fat tissue.

For older individuals and those with significant impairments such as arthritis or peripheral neuropathy, treatment might affect your sense of balance. Be aware of any impairment, and use a cane or walker to reduce the risk for falls and injuries.

The American Cancer Society recommends adult cancer survivors exercise for at least 30 minutes five or more days a week. As you recover and adjust, you might find that more exercise makes you feel even better.

All-Around Good Smoothie

½ cup skim milk

½ cup vanilla nonfat Greek yogurt

½ cup frozen strawberries

½ banana, frozen

1 teaspoon honey

SERVES 1

Place all the ingredients in a blender or food processor and process until smooth; serve.

Also helpful for: N/V

This quick and easy breakfast smoothie is high in calcium and vitamin C.

Nutritional Values

Calories 220, Total Fat 2.5g, Sat Fat 1.5g, Cholesterol 10mg, Sodium 105mg, Carbohydrates 37g, Dietary Fiber 3g, Sugar 26g, Protein 15g, Calcium 20%, Iron 2%, Vitamin C 50%, Vitamin A 6%

Egg-White Crêpes

½ cup whole-wheat flour

1 teaspoon cinnamon

⅛ teaspoon salt

½ cup skim milk

2 large egg whites

1 tablespoon vegetable oil

½ cup frozen mixed berries, thawed and drained

1 tablespoon confectioners' sugar

SERVES 2

1. Whisk together the flour, cinnamon, and salt in a large bowl. In a separate bowl, whisk the milk, egg whites, and oil until thoroughly blended. Pour the milk mixture into the flour mixture and whisk until smooth.

2. Lightly coat a 10-inch skillet with nonstick cooking spray and place over medium heat. Pour ¼ cup of the batter into the skillet. Tilt the pan in a circular motion to allow the batter to spread to the edges. Cook until the bottom is light brown, about 2 minutes. Flip the crêpe over and place 2 tablespoons of the mixed berries on one half; cook for another 2 minutes. Fold the crêpe in half to enclose the berries. Using a spatula, transfer to a serving plate; cover with foil to keep warm.

3. Repeat with the remaining batter and berries to make 3 more crêpes. Dust the filled crêpes with the confectioners' sugar and serve.

Also helpful for: C. N

Nutritional Values

Calories 230, Total Fat 8g, Sat Fat 1g, Cholesterol 0mg, Sodium 230mg, Carbohydrates 34g, Dietary Fiber 5g, Sugar 10g, Protein 10g, Calcium 10%, Iron 8%, Vitamin C 8%, Vitamin A 2%

Light Broccoli Frittata

1 tablespoon olive oil

1 cup chopped onion

2 cups chopped fresh or thawed frozen broccoli (½-inch pieces)

2 garlic cloves, minced

2 teaspoons chopped fresh basil or 1 teaspoon dried

6 large egg whites

Salt and pepper

1 ounce skim milk mozzarella cheese, shredded (¼ cup)

SERVES 2

1. Adjust an oven rack about 6 inches from the broiler element and preheat the broiler. Heat the oil in a large broiler-safe skillet over medium-high heat, add the onions, and cook until softened, about 5 minutes. Add the broccoli, garlic, and basil and continue to cook, stirring occasionally, until the broccoli is bright green and crisp-tender, about 5 minutes.

2. Season the egg whites with salt and pepper to taste and beat with a fork until frothy. Pour the beaten egg whites over the broccoli, tilting the skillet so that they flow evenly throughout the broccoli. Reduce the heat to medium-low, cover, and cook until the egg whites are opaque and almost firm, 3 to 4 minutes.

3. Sprinkle with the mozzarella and place the skillet under the broiler until the cheese melts and begins to brown, 2 to 3 minutes. Cut the frittata in half, sprinkle with additional basil, and serve.

Also helpful for: SM, N

Nutritional Values

Calories 190, Total Fat 8g, Sat Fat 1g, Cholesterol 5mg, Sodium 280mg, Carbohydrates 14g, Dietary Fiber 4g, Sugar 4g, Protein 18g, Calcium 20%, Iron 8%, Vitamin C 120%, Vitamin A 45%

Healthy Breakfast Sandwich

2 tablespoons plain nonfat yogurt

1 tablespoon Dijon mustard

½ teaspoon dried basil

4 large eggs

2 English muffins

4 large tomato slices

½ cup baby spinach leaves

⅛ teaspoon paprika

SERVES 4

1. Adjust an oven rack about 6 inches from the broiler element and preheat the broiler. Whisk together the yogurt, mustard, and basil and set aside. Fill a large skillet almost to the rim with water and bring to a simmer. Add the eggs, cover, and turn the heat to low. Cook until the whites and yolks are set, about 5 minutes.

2. While the eggs are poaching, split the English muffins in half, place on a baking sheet, and broil until lightly toasted.

3. Spread one-quarter of the yogurt mixture on each muffin half. Top each muffin with a tomato slice. Return to the broiler and cook for 1 minute.

4. Top each muffin with one-quarter of the spinach leaves and a poached egg, making sure to let the eggs drain before topping the muffins. Sprinkle with paprika and serve immediately.

Also helpful for: C

Nutritional Values

Calories 170, Total Fat 5g, Sat Fat 1.5g, Cholesterol 185mg, Sodium 420mg, Carbohydrates 22g, Dietary Fiber 4g, Sugar 2g, Protein 11g, Calcium 8%, Iron 20%, Vitamin C 25%, Vitamin A 50%

Mango-Cucumber Salad with Spiced Chicken

Mango-cucumber salad

1 English cucumber, thinly sliced

1 mango, peeled, pitted, and thinly sliced

½ small red onion, finely diced

¼ cup fresh lime juice

¼ cup chopped fresh cilantro

¼ teaspoon cayenne pepper

Spiced chicken

1 pound boneless, skinless chicken breasts, trimmed and cut into thin strips

3 tablespoons garam masala

Salt and pepper

SERVES 4

1. To make the Mango-cucumber salad: Combine all the ingredients in a large bowl and let sit for 30 minutes.

2. To make the Spiced chicken: Sprinkle the chicken pieces on both sides with the garam masala and season with salt and pepper to taste. Spray a large skillet with nonstick cooking spray and heat over medium-high heat. Add the chicken and cook, stirring, until the pieces are browned all over and cooked through, 10 to 15 minutes.

3. Divide the salad among individual plates, top with the chicken, and serve.

Also helpful for: D

This flavorful, colorful salad also tastes great with grilled chicken or with other sources of protein such as hummus or plain yogurt, or it can be served on its own.

Nutritional Values

Calories 200, Total Fat 3.5g, Sat Fat 1g, Cholesterol 75mg, Sodium 135mg, Carbohydrates 17g, Dietary Fiber 2g, Sugar 13g, Protein 25g, Calcium 4%, Iron 4%, Vitamin C 70%, Vitamin A 20%

Soba Noodle Salad

2 tablespoons white miso

⅓ cup water

¼ cup low-sodium soy sauce

2 tablespoons unsweetened apple juice

2 tablespoons toasted sesame oil

2 tablespoons rice vinegar

1 tablespoon grated fresh ginger

2 cups snow peas

1 pound soba noodles

1 cup shredded cooked chicken

2 carrots, peeled and cut into matchsticks (about 1 cup)

⅔ cup chopped scallions

SERVES 4

1. Dissolve the miso in the water. Whisk in the soy sauce, apple juice, sesame oil, vinegar, and ginger.

2. Bring 4 quarts of water to a boil in a large pot. Add the snow peas and cook, uncovered, until tender but still bright green, about 1 minute. Remove the snow peas with a slotted spoon or strainer, place them in a large serving bowl, and set aside.

3. Add the noodles to the boiling water and cook until just tender, about 3 minutes. Drain, rinse under cold water, and drain again. Add the noodles to the bowl with the snow peas, then add the chicken, carrots, and scallions.

4. Rewhisk the sauce, if needed, to combine and pour over the noodles. Toss to coat the noodles and vegetables thoroughly with the sauce, and serve.

Also helpful for: C

Add shredded chicken or diced tofu for protein.

Nutritional Values

Calories 550, Total Fat 10g, Sat Fat 1g, Cholesterol 10mg, Sodium 1600mg, Carbohydrates 92g, Dietary Fiber 9g, Sugar 8g, Protein 25g, Calcium 6%, Iron 25%, Vitamin C 20%, Vitamin A 120%

Cucumber-Mint Salad

2 medium tomatoes, cored and sliced

½ large cucumber, peeled and sliced

2 small oranges, peeled and divided into sections

¼ cup fresh mint leaves

3 tablespoon balsamic vinegar

2 teaspoon olive oil

Salt and pepper

2 tablespoons slivered almonds, toasted

SERVES 4

Combine the tomatoes, cucumber, oranges, and mint in a bowl. Whisk the balsamic vinegar and olive oil together and season with salt and pepper to taste. Pour over the fruit and vegetables, toss to combine, sprinkle with the slivered almonds, and serve.

Also helpful for: N/V

This salad can be made up to 6 hours ahead and refrigerated until needed. Add the almonds just before serving.

Nutritional Values

Calories 100, Total Fat 4.5g, Sat Fat 0g, Cholesterol 0mg, Sodium 5mg, Carbohydrates 13g, Dietary Fiber 2g, Sugar 9g, Protein 2g, Calcium 6%, Iron 4%, Vitamin C 70%, Vitamin A 6%

Creamy Gazpacho

2 cucumbers, peeled, seeded, and chopped

4 scallions, chopped

½ cup chopped fresh parsley, plus extra for garnish

½ jalapeño pepper, seeded and chopped

2 garlic cloves

3 cups tomato-based vegetable juice

1 cup plain yogurt, plus extra for garnish

2 tablespoons fresh lemon juice

Salt and pepper

4 plum tomatoes, cored and chopped

1 orange bell pepper, stemmed, seeded, and chopped

1 yellow bell pepper, stemmed, seeded, and chopped

Hot sauce, such as Tabasco

Tortilla chips (optional)

SERVES 6

1. Pulse 1 cucumber, the scallions, parsley, jalapeño, and garlic in a food processor until very finely chopped. Add the vegetable juice, yogurt, lemon juice, 1/2 teaspoon salt, and ½ teaspoon pepper and process until the mixture is almost smooth but still contains small bits of vegetables.

2. Transfer the mixture to a large bowl and add the remaining cucumber, tomatoes, bell peppers, and hot sauce to taste. Stir well and season with salt and pepper to taste. Cover and refrigerate for 1 hour.

3. Garnish with a dollop of plain yogurt and sprinkle with parsley. Serve with tortilla chips, if using.

Also helpful for: C

Nutritional Values

Calories 90, Total Fat 1g, Sat Fat 0g, Cholesterol 5mg, Sodium 450mg, Carbohydrates 17g, Dietary Fiber 3g, Sugar 9g, Protein 5g, Calcium 10%, Iron 8%, Vitamin C 230%, Vitamin A 45%

Tarragon Leek Soup

1 tablespoon olive oil

2 medium leeks, pale green and white parts only, sliced

2 garlic cloves, minced

1 teaspoon salt

1 tablespoon whole-wheat flour

4 cups vegetable broth

½ cup diced tomato

½ cup tomato juice

⅓ cup finely chopped fresh tarragon

1 tablespoon honey

⅓ cup red wine

SERVES 6

1. Heat the oil in a large saucepan. Add the leeks, garlic, and salt and sauté until the leeks are soft. Stir in the flour and cook, stirring constantly, for 2 to 3 minutes.

2. Slowly whisk the broth into the leeks. Add the tomato and tomato juice, bring to a simmer, and cook until the mixture thickens. Add the tarragon and honey, cover, and cook for 10 minutes. Add the red wine and cook for 1 to 2 minutes; serve immediately.

Also helpful for: N, N/V

You can reduce the sodium in this soup by eliminating the salt and using low-sodium broth. For a thicker soup, add an additional 1 to 2 tablespoons whole-wheat flour. Serve with French bread.

Nutritional Values

Calories 100, Total Fat 3g, Sat Fat 0g, Cholesterol 0mg, Sodium 840mg, Carbohydrates 14g, Dietary Fiber 2g, Sugar 7g, Protein 2g, Calcium 4%, Iron 6%, Vitamin C 20%, Vitamin A 25%

Curried Chickpeas and Tofu

2 tablespoons vegetable oil

1 onion, chopped

1 garlic clove, minced

2 teaspoons ground cumin

1 teaspoon ground coriander

½ teaspoon turmeric

¼ teaspoon pepper

Pinch cayenne (optional)

12 ounces firm or extra-firm tofu, cut into ½-inch cubes

1 (15-ounce) can chickpeas, drained, liquid reserved

2 tomatoes, cored and chopped (about 1 ½ cups)

2 cups frozen peas

Salt

Plain yogurt

Chopped fresh cilantro

SERVES 4

1. Heat the oil in a large skillet over medium-high heat, add the onion and garlic, and cook, stirring, until softened and translucent, about 5 minutes. Add the cumin, coriander, turmeric, pepper, and cayenne, if using, and cook for 1 minute. Add the tofu and cook, stirring constantly, for 1 to 2 minutes.

2. Add the chickpeas and ½ cup of the reserved liquid to the tofu mixture and simmer for 5 minutes. Add the tomatoes and peas, stir, and cook until the mixture is bubbling, about 5 minutes. Season with salt to taste and serve, topped with yogurt and cilantro.

Also helpful for: C

Nutritional Values

Calories 320, Total Fat 13g, Sat Fat 1g, Cholesterol 0mg, Sodium 330mg, Carbohydrates 35g, Dietary Fiber 10g, Sugar 9g, Protein 17g, Calcium 20%, Iron 25%, Vitamin C 45%, Vitamin A 45%

Artichoke Tagine

3 tablespoons olive oil

2 (14-ounce) cans artichoke hearts, patted dry and halved

1 yellow bell pepper, stemmed, seeded, and cut into ¼-inch-wide strips

1 red bell pepper, stemmed, seeded, and cut into ¼-inch-wide strips

1 onion, chopped

4 (3-inch) strips lemon zest plus juice of 1 lemon

8 garlic cloves, minced

2 ½ teaspoons paprika

2 ½ teaspoons garam masala

2 tablespoons all-purpose flour

3 cups vegetable broth

1 tablespoon honey

2 (15-ounce) cans chickpeas, rinsed

½ cup pitted kalamata olives, halved

½ cup chopped pitted dates

⅓ cup plain 2 percent Greek yogurt

½ cup minced fresh cilantro

Salt and pepper

SERVES 6

1. Heat 1 tablespoon of the oil in a Dutch oven over medium heat. Add the artichokes and cook until golden brown, 5 to 7 minutes; transfer to a bowl.

2. Add 1 more tablespoon of the oil to the pot and return to medium heat. Add the bell peppers, onion, and lemon zest strips and cook until the vegetables are softened and lightly browned, 5 to 7 minutes.

3. Add the garlic, paprika, and garam masala and cook until fragrant, about 30 seconds. Stir in the flour and cook for 1 minute. Slowly stir in the vegetable broth and honey, scraping up any browned bits and smoothing out any lumps.

4. Stir in the browned artichokes, chickpeas, olives, and dates and bring to a simmer. Reduce the heat to medium-low, cover, and cook, stirring occasionally, until the liquid has thickened slightly and the vegetables are tender, about 15 minutes.

5. Remove from the heat and remove the lemon zest strips. Stir ½ cup of the liquid from the pot into the yogurt and then stir the yogurt mixture back into the pot. Stir in the remaining oil, the cilantro, and lemon juice. Season with salt and pepper to taste and serve, topped with yogurt and fresh cilantro, if desired.

Also helpful for: C, N

Serve this colorful, nutritious one-pot meal with couscous, rice, or farro.

This vegetarian meal can easily be made vegan by leaving out the yogurt.

Nutritional Values

Calories 320, Total Fat 9g, Sat Fat 1g, Cholesterol 0mg, Sodium 1000mg, Carbohydrates 52g, Dietary Fiber 10g, Sugar 20g, Protein 10g, Calcium 6%, Iron 10%, Vitamin C 160%, Vitamin A 30%

Miso-Glazed Cod

6 (6-ounce) cod or black cod fillets

⅓ cup dark miso

¼ cup packed dark brown sugar

2 tablespoons low-sodium soy sauce

1 teaspoon toasted sesame oil

Toasted sesame seeds

SERVES 6

1. Adjust one oven rack about 6 inches from the broiler element and a second rack to the middle position. Preheat the broiler. Rinse the cod and pat dry with paper towels; arrange on a baking sheet. Stir the miso, sugar, soy sauce, and sesame oil together in a small bowl until the sugar is fully dissolved.

2. Brush about 1 tablespoon miso glaze on each fish fillet. Broil the fillets until the tops are slightly charred and the glaze has caramelized, 3 to 4 minutes. Remove the fish from the oven and brush with the remaining glaze. Lower the oven temperature to 375 degrees, return the fish to the lower oven rack, and cook just until flaky, 5 to 6 minutes. Sprinkle with sesame seeds and serve.

Also helpful for: SM, N

Braised baby bok choy makes an excellent accompaniment to the cod.

Nutritional Values

Calories 210, Total Fat 2.5g, Sat Fat 0g, Cholesterol 75mg, Sodium 940mg, Carbohydrates 12g, Dietary Fiber 0g, Sugar 11g, Protein 32g, Calcium 4%, Iron 4%, Vitamin C 4%, Vitamin A 2%

Succotash with Grilled Scallops and Parsley Drizzle

Parsley drizzle

1 cup lightly packed parsley leaves

2 tablespoons extra-virgin olive oil

2 tablespoons water, plus extra as needed

1 tablespoon fresh lemon juice

Succotash and scallops

1 tablespoon olive oil

1 small onion, chopped

2 garlic cloves, minced

2 ½ cups frozen corn kernels, thawed

1 (10-ounce) package frozen lima beans, thawed

1 pint grape tomatoes, halved

1 zucchini (about 8 ounces) quartered lengthwise and sliced

¼ cup chopped fresh basil

1 tablespoon cider vinegar

Salt and pepper

1 ¼ pounds large sea scallops (about 16); tendons removed

SERVES 4

1. To make the Parsley drizzle: Place all the ingredients in a blender and process until smooth, adding water as needed for a pourable consistency.

2. To make the Succotash and scallops: Heat 2 teaspoons of the oil in a large skillet over medium heat. Add the onion and cook, stirring occasionally, until softened, about 2 minutes. Add the garlic and cook for 1 minute. Stir in the corn, lima beans, tomatoes, and zucchini and cook, stirring occasionally, until the vegetables are tender and begin to release liquid, about 7 minutes. Remove from the heat, stir in the basil and vinegar, and season with salt and pepper to taste. Cover to keep warm.

3. Heat the remaining teaspoon oil in a large nonstick skillet over medium-high heat. Pat the scallops dry and season them with ¼ teaspoon salt and ¼ teaspoon pepper. Add the scallops to the hot pan and cook until browned on both sides, about 3 minutes. Divide the succotash and scallops onto plates, drizzle the parsley drizzle over the scallops, and serve.

Also helpful for: C. N

Nutritional Values

Calories 390, Total Fat 11g, Sat Fat 1.5g, Cholesterol 35mg, Sodium 930mg, Carbohydrates 46g, Dietary Fiber 9g, Sugar 5g, Protein 27g, Calcium 8%, Iron 20%, Vitamin C 100%, Vitamin A 45%

Spicy Bison Burgers

Horseradish mayo

½ cup light mayonnaise

1 tablespoon creamed horseradish

1 teaspoon fresh lemon juice

1 teaspoon Dijon mustard

Burgers

1 tablespoon olive oil

3 celery ribs, chopped

½ onion, chopped

2 tablespoons tomato paste

1 garlic clove, minced

1 pound ground bison

2 tablespoons Worcestershire sauce

½ teaspoon celery salt

¼ teaspoon hot sauce, such as Tabasco4 whole-wheat hamburger buns

Diced tomato and sliced onion, for garnish

SERVES 4

1. To make the Horseradish mayo: Whisk all the ingredients together and refrigerate until needed.

2. To make the Burgers: Preheat a charcoal or gas grill. Heat the oil in a medium skillet over medium heat. Add the celery, onion, tomato paste, and garlic and cook, stirring, until the vegetables are softened, about 5 minutes. Transfer the mixture to a large bowl and let cool slightly.

3. Add the ground bison, Worcestershire sauce, celery salt, and hot sauce to the vegetables and stir to mix thoroughly. Divide the mixture into four equal portions and shape into patties.

4. Grill the burgers until they register 165 degrees, flipping several times to cook through. Place the burgers on the buns, top with horseradish mayo and/or other favorite toppings and serve.

Also helpful for: N

Nutritional Values

Calories 550, Total Fat 34g, Sat Fat 2.5g, Cholesterol 90mg, Sodium 810mg, Carbohydrates 34g, Dietary Fiber 6g, Sugar 9g, Protein 26g, Calcium 10%, Iron 30%, Vitamin C 25%, Vitamin A 10%

NEUTROPENIA

Sometimes going through cancer treatment can cause a condition known as neutropenia. Neutropenia is a disorder characterized by an abnormally low white blood cell count. White blood cells are cells that are continually being formed in the bone marrow; they are susceptible to some chemotherapy drugs, which are designed to target rapidly growing cells. White blood cells are necessary to fight off bacterial infections, and too few can cause a suppressed immune system, which is associated with a high risk for foodborne illness. If you've been told that you are neutropenic, we have some basic guidelines that can help you avoid a food-based infection.

Because there is no guarantee that restaurants always follow safe practices, if you are neutropenic, it is best to focus on eating foods made at home. Long food transit time—the time it takes food to get from the farm to the table—can easily promote bacterial growth. You don't know how long something took to get to the store, but you have control over the time you or a family member spends transporting and preparing food. In general, whether at home or at a restaurant, well-cooked food is less likely to be contaminated, and food should be eaten as soon as it is cooked. Here are some tips to ensure safe food preparation:

> Wash hands well before handling food, and again after touching raw meats and eggs. Be careful of contaminating work areas like the sink, faucets, and utensils while you are working around the kitchen.

> Use one cutting board for vegetables and fruits and a separate one for meats. (Synthetic materials are best, and wash them in a dishwasher).

> Discard leftover foods 24 hours after preparation.

> Cool hot foods quickly in a refrigerated ice bath to avoid bacterial growth.

Foods to avoid:

Dairy: raw (unpasteurized) milk, yogurt, soft cheeses with molds (such as Brie and Roquefort), sharp cheddar, feta cheese, farmer's cheese

Meats and proteins: raw or undercooked meat, poultry, fish, and game; deli meats; and processed meats such as hot dogs, pâté, and meat spreads; smoked and pickled fish or meats; tempeh; raw tofu; raw or undercooked eggs

Fruits and vegetables: unroasted raw nuts and roasted nuts in the shell; unpasteurized juices; raw sprouts, items from salad bars, and commercial salsas

Grains: uncooked grains (cereals are usually toasted or cooked), any items from self-serve bins.

Beverages: well water, cold-brewed tea, mate tea

Desserts: unrefrigerated cream-filled pastry products

Other: salad dressings with aged or blue cheese, miso soup, raw honey, herbal supplement preparations, brewers yeast

Hash Browns with Sausage and Oven-Roasted Tomatoes

1 ½ pounds russet potatoes, peeled and chopped

4 tablespoons (2 ounces) butter

1 large onion, finely chopped

Salt and pepper

8 ounces sausage, crumbled

2 tablespoons olive oil

2 cups cherry tomatoes

1 tablespoon balsamic vinegar

SERVES 4

1. Adjust two oven racks to the upper-middle and lower-middle positions. Preheat the oven to 400 degrees. Place the potatoes and ½ teaspoon salt in a large saucepan and cover with water by 1 inch. Bring to a boil and cook until almost tender, about 10 minutes. Drain the potatoes, return them to the pot and mash them coarsely.

2. Melt the butter in a large nonstick skillet over medium-low heat, add the onion, and cook, stirring occasionally, until soft and golden, about 15 minutes. Add the potatoes and season with salt and pepper to taste. Cook, stirring and mashing the potatoes occasionally, until well browned and crisp around the edges, 15 to 20 minutes.

3. Meanwhile, spread the crumbled sausage in a roasting pan, drizzle with 1 tablespoon of the oil, and cook on the lower rack for 25 minutes.

Spread the tomatoes in a shallow baking dish and drizzle with the remaining 1 tablespoon oil. When the sausage has been in the oven for 5 minutes, place the tomatoes on the upper rack. Cook the tomatoes for 15 minutes; drizzle with the balsamic vinegar, then return to the oven and cook for 5 minutes.

4. Spoon the hash browns onto plates and top with the sausage, the tomatoes, and their juices. Serve.

Also helpful for: WLP

Nutritional Values

Calories 500, Total Fat 34g, Sat Fat 13g, Cholesterol 70mg, Sodium 380mg, Carbohydrates 38g, Dietary Fiber 4g, Sugar 5g, Protein 13g, Calcium 4%, Iron 15%, Vitamin C 40%, Vitamin A 20%

Warm Compote with Peaches, Nectarines, and Apricots

2 oranges

2 tablespoons sugar

1 cinnamon stick

2 pounds peaches, nectarines, and apricots

2 cups vanilla yogurt

SERVES 4

1. With a vegetable peeler, remove the zest from 1 orange, being careful not to remove the white pith. Slice the zest into thin strips and place in a medium saucepan. Juice both oranges and add the juice to the saucepan. Add the sugar and cinnamon stick and heat over low heat, stirring, until the sugar dissolves.

2. Peel, halve, and pit the peaches, then cut them into slices. Halve, pit, and slice the nectarines. Halve and pit the apricots. Add the peaches, nectarines, and apricots to the pan with orange juice mixture, cover, and simmer gently until the fruit is softened, 4 to 5 minutes.

3. Serve the compote warm with the vanilla yogurt.

Also helpful for: SM, C

For a textural contrast, sprinkle granola over the compote and yogurt. Try this compote stirred into oatmeal or spooned over ice cream.

Nutritional Values

Calories 280, Total Fat 2.5g, Sat Fat 1g, Cholesterol 10mg, Sodium 75mg, Carbohydrates 60g, Dietary Fiber 4g, Sugar 42g, Protein 6g, Calcium 20%, Iron 4%, Vitamin C 70%, Vitamin A 60%

Baked Oatmeal with Raspberries

2 ¾ cups 2 percent milk

4 large eggs

¼ cup maple syrup

2 teaspoons salt

1 teaspoon ground cinnamon

4 cups old-fashioned oats

1 cup raspberries

SERVES 6

1. Preheat the oven to 350 degrees. Spray an 8-inch square baking dish with nonstick cooking spray. Whisk together the milk, eggs, syrup, salt, and cinnamon in a large bowl. Add the oats and whisk to blend. (The mixture will be very wet.)

2. Spoon the mixture into the prepared baking dish and sprinkle the raspberries evenly over the top, then press them gently with the back of a spoon until they are just submerged. Bake the oatmeal until lightly browned, 25 to 30 minutes. Serve warm.

Also helpful for: C. WLP. N/V

Nutritional Values

Calories 330, Total Fat 9g, Sat Fat 3g, Cholesterol 140mg, Sodium 880mg, Carbohydrates 49g, Dietary Fiber 6g, Sugar 11g, Protein 15g, Calcium 15%, Iron 15%, Vitamin C 6%, Vitamin A 6%

Mediterranean Split Pea Soup

1 tablespoon plus 2 teaspoons extra-virgin olive oil

1 large onion, chopped

2–3 cups water

2 cups vegetable broth

1 cup green split peas

Salt and pepper

2 slices mild onion, such as Vidalia

SERVES 2

1. Heat 1 tablespoon of the oil in a large saucepan over medium heat, add the chopped onion, and cook, stirring, until translucent and just beginning to brown, about 10 minutes.

2. Add 2 cups of the water, the broth, and split peas and bring to a boil. Reduce the heat and simmer until the peas are tender and mushy, 45 to 60 minutes, adding up to 1 cup additional water, for a thick yet pourable consistency. Season the soup with salt and pepper to taste. Divide into bowls and top each portion with an onion slice and a teaspoon of olive oil. Serve.

Also helpful for: SM. C. WGP

Served with a loaf of hearty bread, this simple soup makes a light, yet nourishing, dinner.

Nutritional Values

Calories 420, Total Fat 7g, Sat Fat 0.5g, Cholesterol 0mg, Sodium 480mg, Carbohydrates 70g, Dietary Fiber 34g, Sugar 8g, Protein 22g, Calcium 6%, Iron 15%, Vitamin C 15%, Vitamin A 20%

Turkey-Bean Chili

1 pound ground turkey

1 onion, chopped

1 garlic clove, minced

¼ cup chili powder

1 teaspoon ground cumin

Salt and pepper

1 ½ cups plus 2 tablespoons low-sodium chicken broth

1 (15-ounce) can black beans, drained and rinsed

1 (15-ounce) can kidney beans, drained and rinsed

1 (14.5-ounce) can diced tomatoes

1 cup frozen corn kernels

SERVES 6

1. Spray a Dutch oven with nonstick cooking spray, add the turkey, onion, and garlic, and cook over medium-high heat, stirring frequently to break up any clumps of turkey, until the turkey is cooked through. Add the chili powder, cumin, ⅛ teaspoon salt and ½ teaspoon pepper and cook, stirring, about 5 minutes.

2. Gradually add the broth, stirring to loosen any browned bits from the bottom of the pot. Add the black beans, kidney beans, tomatoes with their juice, and corn. Bring the mixture to a simmer and cook for 15 minutes. Season with salt to taste and serve.

Also helpful for: C. WGP

To lower the sodium in this dish, you can substitute 1 ½ cups cooked dried black beans and 1 ½ cups cooked dried kidney beans for the canned beans.

Nutritional Values

Calories 280, Total Fat 6g, Sat Fat 1.5g, Cholesterol 50mg, Sodium 840mg, Carbohydrates 31g, Dietary Fiber 8g, Sugar 5g, Protein 24g, Calcium 8%, Iron 15%, Vitamin C 20%, Vitamin A 20%

Vegetable Lasagna

1 (19-ounce) package frozen chopped spinach or broccoli, thawed and squeezed dry

1 pound (2 cups) ricotta cheese

1 ounce Parmesan cheese, grated (½ cup), plus extra for garnish

½ teaspoon Italian herbs

1 (32-ounce) jar spaghetti sauce

9 lasagna noodles, cooked and drained, or no-boil noodles

SERVES 10

1. Combine the spinach, ricotta, Parmesan, and Italian herbs.

2. Spread about 1 cup of the sauce in the bottom of a 9 x 13-inch baking pan, arrange 3 noodles on the sauce, and then spoon half of the spinach filling evenly over the noodles. Repeat with 1 cup more sauce, 3 more noodles, and the remaining filling. Layer the remaining 3 noodles over the filling, spread the remaining sauce over the noodles, and sprinkle with extra Parmesan.

3. Bake until the mixture is bubbling and the cheese is lightly browned, about 30 minutes. Let cool 5 to 10 minutes, then serve.

Also helpful for: C. WGP

This dish is easy to adapt to your dietary needs; low-sodium and vegetarian sauces are available, and you can try low-fat ricotta.

Nutritional Values

Calories 250, Total Fat 8g, Sat Fat 4.5g, Cholesterol 25mg, Sodium 720mg, Carbohydrates 31g, Dietary Fiber 3g, Sugar 8g, Protein 13g, Calcium 40%, Iron 15%,, Vitamin C 10%, Vitamin A 45%

Pan-Seared Portobello Mushrooms

2 tablespoons red wine

2 tablespoons low-sodium soy sauce

1 tablespoon balsamic vinegar

2 garlic cloves, minced

½ teaspoon dried oregano

4 large portobello mushrooms, stems removed

SERVES 4

1. Combine the wine, soy sauce, vinegar, garlic, and oregano in a large skillet over high heat and cook until the mixture begins to bubble.

2. Add the mushrooms, gill side up. Lower the heat to medium, cover, and cook for 3 minutes. If the pan becomes dry, add 2 to 3 tablespoons water.

3. Turn the mushrooms over, cover, and cook until they are tender when pierced with a sharp knife, about 5 minutes. Serve.

Also helpful for: WGP, D

Stored in a covered container in the refrigerator, leftover cooked mushrooms will keep for up to 3 days.

Nutritional Values

Calories 45, Total Fat 0g, Sat Fat 0g, Cholesterol 0mg, Sodium 290mg, Carbohydrates 6g, Dietary Fiber 1g, Sugar 2g, Protein 2g, Calcium 2%, Iron 4%, Vitamin C 2%, Vitamin A 0%

Italian Braised Chicken and Fennel

4 tomatoes, cored and finely chopped

1 garlic clove, minced

¼ cup white wine

2 teaspoons balsamic vinegar

Salt and pepper

4 skinless chicken breasts

4 small fennel bulbs, trimmed, cored, and cut into quarters

Chopped fresh parsley

SERVES 4

1. Combine the tomatoes, garlic, wine, vinegar, and salt and pepper to taste in a large nonstick skillet and bring to a boil. Reduce the heat and add the chicken and fennel pieces. Cover and simmer until the chicken and fennel are tender, about 30 minutes.

2. Using a slotted spoon, transfer the chicken and fennel to warm plates. Cover to keep warm. Bring the sauce to a boil and cook, stirring occasionally, until thickened slightly, about 5 minutes. Spoon the sauce over the chicken, sprinkle with parsley, and serve.

Also helpful for: WGP

Nutritional Values

Calories 260, Total Fat 4g, Sat Fat 0.5g, Cholesterol 75mg, Sodium 270mg, Carbohydrates 25g, Dietary Fiber 9g, Sugar 5g, Protein 30g, Calcium 15%, Iron 15%, Vitamin C 90%, Vitamin A 35%

Braised Chicken with Shallots and Dried Fruit

8 boneless, skinless chicken breasts, trimmed

Salt and pepper

3 tablespoons olive oil

½ cup water

4 bay leaves

½ red onion, cut into ¼-inch rounds

⅔ cup dry red wine

3 tablespoons champagne vinegar

8 dates, pitted and chopped

4 dried apricot halves, quartered

SERVES 8

1. Pat the chicken dry and season with salt and pepper to taste.

2. Heat the oil in a Dutch oven over medium-high heat. Add the chicken and cook until browned on both sides, 7 to 10 minutes on each side. Add the water and bay leaves, cover, and reduce the heat to low. Cook for 15 minutes.

3. Transfer the chicken to a plate and cover to keep warm. Pour the liquid into a small bowl, discard the bay leaves, and set aside. Add the onions to the pot, increase the heat to medium, and cook until they begin to soften and color, about 5 minutes. Add the red wine and vinegar and stir to scrape up any browned bits from the bottom of the pot. Add the dates and apricots.

Return the chicken to the pot, pour the reserved liquid over the top, and simmer until the chicken is heated through and tender, about 20 minutes. Serve.

Also helpful for: C, WGP

Leftovers can be frozen.

For extra fiber (to alleviate constipation) increase the amount of dates and apricots as desired.

Nutritional Values

Calories 240, Total Fat 8g, Sat Fat 1.5g, Cholesterol 75mg, Sodium 140mg, Carbohydrates 10g, Dietary Fiber 1g, Sugar 7g, Protein 25g, Calcium 2%, Iron 4%, Vitamin C 4%, Vitamin A 4%

Chicken Morsels with Peppers

2 large yellow bell peppers

2 large red bell peppers

1 ¼ pounds boneless, skinless chicken breasts, trimmed and cut into bite-sized pieces

Salt and pepper

¼ cup olive oil

1 onion, chopped

6 garlic cloves, minced

2 large tomatoes, peeled, seeded and cut into strips, juices reserved

Paprika (optional)

SERVES 4

1. Adjust an oven rack about 6 inches from the broiler element and preheat the broiler. Arrange the bell peppers on a broiler pan and broil until blackened and blistered, turning to blacken all sides. Transfer the peppers to a bowl, cover, and let cool for about 10 minutes. Peel off the skins, remove the stems and seeds, and cut the peppers into wide strips; set aside.

2. Season the chicken with salt and pepper to taste. Heat the olive oil in a large skillet over high heat. Add the chicken and brown on all sides. Reduce the heat to medium-low and add the peppers, tomatoes and their juices, onion, and garlic. Sprinkle with paprika, if using. Cook until the chicken is tender, 15 to 20 minutes. Transfer to a warmed platter and serve.

Also helpful for: WGP

Nutritional Values

Calories 380, Total Fat 18g, Sat Fat 3g, Cholesterol 90mg, Sodium 180mg, Carbohydrates 19g, Dietary Fiber 4g, Sugar 7g, Protein 33g, Calcium 4%, Iron 10%, Vitamin C 490%, Vitamin A 70%

Stir-Fried Beef and Snow Peas

1 pound round or sirloin steak, trimmed and thinly sliced

5 tablespoons hoisin sauce

2 tablespoons low-sodium soy sauce

2 tablespoons dry sherry

1 pound snow peas, trimmed

1 (15 ounce) can of whole baby corn

1 onion, thinly sliced

1 carrot, peeled and thinly sliced

1 garlic clove, minced

1 teaspoon minced fresh ginger

1 (8-ounce) can water chestnuts

1 cup cooked rice or noodles

SERVES 4

1. Combine the beef, hoisin sauce, soy sauce, and sherry in a bowl and set aside.

2. Spray a large skillet with nonstick cooking spray and heat over medium-high heat. Add the snow peas, baby corn, onion, carrot, garlic, and ginger and cook, stirring, until softened, about 5 minutes.

3. Add the beef and marinade mixture to the wok and cook, stirring, until tender, 2 to 3 minutes. Add the water chestnuts and cook until heated through, 1 minute. Serve.

Also helpful for: WGP

Nutritional Values

Calories 400, Total Fat 9g, Sat Fat 3g, Cholesterol 55mg, Sodium 950mg, Carbohydrates 47g, Dietary Fiber 9g, Sugar 14g, Protein 27g, Calcium 8%, Iron 25%, Vitamin C 60%, Vitamin A 80%

Roast Pork Loin with Root Vegetables

1 (3 ½-pound) boned, pork loin, trimmed, rolled, and tied

4 garlic cloves, slivered

12 sage leaves, thinly sliced, plus sage sprigs for garnish

Salt and pepper

2 pounds turnips (about 12 small), trimmed, peeled, and cut in quarters

1 pound red potatoes (about 6 small), cut into ½-inch pieces

1 pound carrots, peeled and cut into 2-inch pieces

2 tablespoons olive oil

2 teaspoons unsalted butter, softened

½ cup red or white wine

½ cup low-sodium chicken broth

Pinch sugar (optional)

SERVES 8

1. Preheat the oven to 500 degrees. With the tip of a paring knife, make a ¼-inch slit in the pork loin and insert a garlic sliver and a strip of sage. Repeat at regular intervals, making rows all around the loin. Season the meat with salt and pepper and place it in a large, heavy roasting pan.

2. Place the turnips, potatoes, and carrots in a large bowl with the olive oil, season with salt and pepper to taste, and toss until the vegetables are coated. Pour the vegetables over the loin, turning the meat so that it is coated with oil. Arrange the vegetables in a single layer around the meat, with cut side down. Roast for 30 minutes, turning the vegetables over and basting the meat with pan juices halfway through cooking. Remove the roasting pan from the oven. Loosen the meat and smear the top with the butter; stir the vegetables. Return to the oven and roast until the meat registers 145 degrees, about 10 minutes. (The meat may be slightly pink.)

3. Remove the strings from the roast and transfer it to a carving board; tent with aluminum foil. Transfer the vegetables to a bowl and cover to keep warm.

4. Place the roasting pan over medium-high heat. Add the wine and stir to loosen any browned bits in the pan. Add the broth and cook until reduced by half. Season with salt and sugar to taste, then strain into a sauce boat or bowl.

5. Remove the strings from the roast and slice it. Transfer the sliced roast to a serving platter, spoon the vegetables around the meat, and garnish with sage sprigs. Serve, passing the sauce separately.

Also helpful for: C, N/V

Nutritional Values

Calories 430, Total Fat 11g, Sat Fat 3g,
Cholesterol 130mg, Sodium 220mg,
Carbohydrates 33g, Dietary Fiber 5g, Sugar
9g, Protein 45g, Calcium 6%, Iron 20%,
Vitamin C 60%, Vitamin A 200%

Baked Apple Pudding

½ cup low-fat cottage cheese

¼ cup packed light brown sugar

1 teaspoon ground cinnamon

1 cup 1 percent low-fat milk

1 pound cooking apples, such as Cortlands, peeled, cored, and chopped into ½-inch pieces

4 ounces whole-wheat bread, crusts removed, cut into ½-inch pieces

2 tablespoons golden raisins

SERVES 4

1. Preheat the oven to 425 degrees. In a large bowl, stir together the cottage cheese, 3 tablespoons of the sugar, and the cinnamon. Stir in the milk. Add the apples, bread, and raisins and stir to combine. Turn the mixture into a 9-inch square baking dish and sprinkle with the remaining 1 tablespoon sugar.

2. Set the baking dish on a sheet pan and bake for 35 minutes. (Cover with a piece of aluminum foil, if necessary, to prevent overbrowning during the last 10 minutes.) Serve hot.

Also helpful for: SM, C, WGP, N/V

This pudding can be topped with the topping mixture from the Ginger-Rhubarb Crunch (page 50). Sprinkle the topping evenly over the pudding. Bake uncovered for the entire baking time.

Nutritional Values

Calories 250, Total Fat 1.5g, Sat Fat 0.5g, Cholesterol 5mg, Sodium 260mg, Carbohydrates 53g, Dietary Fiber 5g, Sugar 35g, Protein 9g, Calcium 15%, Iron 2%, Vitamin C 10%, Vitamin A 4%

NAUSEA AND VOMITING

Feeling sick to your stomach can make eating and drinking very challenging throughout treatment. The vomiting reflex evolved as a necessary mechanism to protect animals from eating dangerous or spoiled foods, so it is a healthy human function. Obviously, however, when triggered repeatedly it can be harmful, causing pain and dehydration.

The physical sources of nausea and vomiting are complicated; often there is more than one contributing factor but sometimes there are no obvious causes. Nausea can be a side effect of cancer or its treatment, including chemotherapy and radiation therapy. Drugs are carried by the bloodstream into the brain, where their presence is interpreted as evidence of something potentially poisonous in the stomach—so the brain instructs the stomach to empty itself out. Most of the effective antiemetic agents (drugs to prevent nausea and vomiting) work in the brain to stop this reflex. Sometimes nausea is instead due to a physical problem with the stomach's muscular activity, leading to a sensation of pressure on the intestine, or even acting like a blockage. Pain, fatigue, medications, and even emotional stress can also cause nausea. It's important to understand the source of your nausea in order to treat it appropriately, and to look for more than one possible cause. In the meantime, focus on getting enough nutrition to improve your energy, manage the nausea, and provide a better quality of life.

Keep in mind that talking to your doctors about anti-nausea medication is a very important part of treatment. Be sure to communicate about what works and what doesn't. And remember that nausea and vomiting are actually two different, although related, things. Just because you are not vomiting doesn't mean that the nausea is gone. Nausea by itself is obviously uncomfortable, leads to a poor appetite, and can usually be prevented.

Food and fluids can often be very helpful to manage nausea, but finding the motivation to eat is often a big problem. It may be helpful to talk to your family members or caregivers about what side effects you expect during treatment and tell them that you may need help with preparing nutritional foods on difficult days. Ask them to help with grocery shopping and meal preparation ahead of time.

Here are some ways to make the eating process easier:

Focus on eating five to six small portions per day instead of larger meals.

Eat ready-prepared foods that do not have a lot of odor. Food smells can sometimes avert an appetite.

Eat foods that are bland, such as crackers, chicken soup, and unsweetened hot cereal.

Avoid spicy, greasy, and sweet foods; these can perpetuate the nausea.

Drink enough fluids. Sip on sports drinks, chicken broth, warm water, and mild fruit juices, and eat popsicles throughout the day. Ginger tea and ginger ale may also be helpful for hydration and managing nausea.

Try to relax. Stress can make nausea worse. Sitting in your favorite chair, reading a book, or meditating can be helpful for stress.

Foods to try:

Dairy: yogurt

Meats and other proteins: eggs (scrambled), boiled or baked meat, fish, and poultry

Fruits and vegetables: potatoes, non-acidic fruits like apples, cantaloupe, and berries

Grains: soda crackers, bagels, plain noodles, rice, toast, and cold cereal with low-fat milk

Beverages: vegetable juices and smoothies made with non-acidic fruits and low-fat dairy

Other: soups made with low-fat milk

Peach Pie Smoothie

1 cup frozen sliced peaches

½ cup 1 percent low-fat milk

½ cup plain nonfat yogurt

1 tablespoon honey, plus more to taste

¼ teaspoon vanilla extract

⅛ teaspoon ground cinnamon

⅛ teaspoon grated nutmeg

⅛ teaspoon ground ginger

SERVES 1

Place all the ingredients in a blender and blend
until smooth; serve.

Also helpful for: SM, WGP, N

Nutritional Values

Calories 240, Total Fat 1.5g, Sat Fat 1g,
Cholesterol 10mg, Sodium 180mg,
Carbohydrates 48g, Dietary Fiber 2g, Sugar
43g, Protein 14g, Calcium 35%, Iron 2%,
Vitamin C 210%, Vitamin A 15%

Ginger Ale Pumpkin Bread

2 cups all-purpose flour

1 cup whole-wheat flour

2 teaspoons baking powder

1 teaspoon pumpkin pie spice

1 teaspoon ground cinnamon

1 teaspoon grated nutmeg

½ teaspoon ground ginger

¼ teaspoon ground cloves

¼ teaspoon salt

½ cup pumpkin purée

¼ cup packed brown sugar

3 tablespoons vegetable oil

1 ½ cups ginger ale (not diet)

SERVES 10

1. Preheat the oven to 350 degrees. Grease a 9 x 5-inch loaf pan. Whisk together the all-purpose flour, whole-wheat flour, baking powder, pumpkin pie spice, cinnamon, nutmeg, ginger, cloves, and salt.

2. In a large bowl, beat together the pumpkin purée, brown sugar, and oil. Add the flour mixture and stir briefly, then pour in the ginger ale and mix until just combined.

3. Scrape the batter into the prepared loaf pan. Bake until the top is firm to the touch, the loaf pulls away from the sides of the pan, and a cake tester inserted in the center comes out clean, 55 to 60 minutes. Let the loaf cool in the pan on a wire rack for 10 minutes, then turn out onto the rack and let cool completely.

Also helpful for: SM, N

Nutritional Values

Calories 220, Total Fat 5g, Sat Fat 0.5g, Cholesterol 0mg, Sodium 200mg, Carbohydrates 41g, Dietary Fiber 3g, Sugar 9g, Protein 4g, Calcium 4%, Iron 10%, Vitamin C 0%, Vitamin A 20%

Easy Breakfast Rice Pudding

2 ¼ cups water

1 cup long-grain brown rice

2 cups whole milk

½ cup chopped almonds

¼ cup maple syrup

1 teaspoon ground cinnamon

¼ cup raisins (optional)

SERVES 2 TO 3

1. Combine the water and rice in a medium saucepan, bring to a boil, cover, reduce the heat, and simmer until the rice is tender and all the water is absorbed, 40 to 50 minutes.

2. Add the milk, almonds, maple syrup, and cinnamon and return to a boil. Reduce the heat and simmer, stirring occasionally, until the desired consistency is reached, 5 to 8 minutes. Stir in the raisins, if using, and serve.

Also helpful for: SM, N

Soymilk or rice milk may be used in place of the milk in this recipe.

Nutritional Values

Calories 490, Total Fat 16g, Sat Fat 4g, Cholesterol 15mg, Sodium 85mg, Carbohydrates 75g, Dietary Fiber 6g, Sugar 25g, Protein 14g, Calcium 30%, Iron 10%, Vitamin C 0%, Vitamin A 6%

Soft Granola Bars

2 cups old-fashioned or quick-cooking oats

1 ½ cups all-purpose flour

1 ½ teaspoons ground cinnamon

1 teaspoon baking soda

½ teaspoon ground allspice

¼ teaspoon salt

1 cup packed brown sugar

1 cup unsweetened applesauce

2 large eggs

2 teaspoons vanilla extract

1 cup raisins or chopped pitted dates

1 cup chopped walnuts, pecans, or almonds (optional)

¼ cup honey

2 tablespoons (1 ounce) unsalted butter

MAKES 36 BARS

1. Preheat the oven to 350 degrees. Grease a 10 ½ x 15 ½-inch jelly roll pan. Combine the oats, flour, cinnamon, baking soda, allspice, and salt in a bowl.

2. Mix the sugar, applesauce, eggs, and vanilla in a large bowl with spoon until smooth. Add the oat mixture to the sugar mixture and stir to combine. Stir in the dates and nuts, if using. Scrape the mixture into the prepared pan and smooth the surface by pressing with a spatula. Bake until the center is set but not firm, 17 to 22 minutes. Let the bars cool in the pan on a wire rack.

3. Heat the honey and butter in a small saucepan over medium heat, stirring constantly, until the butter is melted and the mixture is heated through. Drizzle the glaze over the bars and let cool completely, then cut the bars.

Also helpful for: C. N

Nutritional Values

Calories 100, Total Fat 1.5g, Sat Fat 0g, Cholesterol 10mg, Sodium 60mg, Carbohydrates 20g, Dietary Fiber 1g, Sugar 12g, Protein 2g, Calcium 2%, Iron 4%, Vitamin C 0%, Vitamin A 0%

Whole-Wheat Blueberry Pancakes

1 ¼ cups whole-wheat flour

2 teaspoons baking powder

¼ teaspoon salt

1 ¼ cups skim milk

1 large egg

2 tablespoons honey

1 cup blueberries

Vegetable oil

Maple syrup, warmed

MAKES 10 PANCAKES; SERVES 5

1. Whisk the flour, baking powder, and salt together in a bowl. In a separate bowl, whisk together the milk, egg, and honey. Stir in the flour mixture until just moistened; add the blueberries and stir to incorporate.

2. Heat a large nonstick skillet over medium heat, or heat a nonstick electric griddle to 375 degrees. (The skillet is ready when drops of water splashed on the surface bounce and sizzle.) Lightly oil the pan. Using a ¼-cup measure, ladle the batter onto the griddle to form 4-inch cakes. Cook until the bottoms are browned and bubbles appear on the surface. Flip the pancakes over and continue to cook about 2 minutes. Repeat with the remaining batter and serve with warmed maple syrup.

Also helpful for: SM, WGP, N

Bite-sized pieces of any fruit, such as banana chunks or raspberries, can be used in place of the blueberries.

Nutritional Values

Calories 190, Total Fat 1.5g, Sat Fat 0g, Cholesterol 35mg, Sodium 500mg, Carbohydrates 37g, Dietary Fiber 4g, Sugar 13g, Protein 8g, Calcium 10%, Iron 8%, Vitamin C 6%, Vitamin A 4%

Chicken Noodle Soup

6 cups low-sodium chicken broth

12 ounces boneless, skinless chicken breasts, trimmed

2 leeks, white parts only, sliced

1 carrot, peeled and thinly sliced

1 garlic clove, minced (optional)

1 tablespoon fresh chopped parsley

1 teaspoon dried basil

12 ounces small-size pasta, like ditalini or mini farfalle

Salt

SERVES 6

1. Combine the broth, chicken, leeks, carrot, garlic, if using, parsley, and basil in a Dutch oven. Bring to a boil, then reduce the heat, cover, and simmer until the chicken is completely cooked, about 15 minutes. Remove the chicken, let cool slightly, then shred into bite-sized pieces.

2. Add the mini farfalle to the broth mixture and cook until the noodles are almost tender, about 5 minutes. Return the chicken to the pot and cook until the chicken is heated through and the noodles are tender. Season with salt to taste and serve.

Also helpful for: SM, N

Chicken Noodle Soup can be prepared ahead of time and frozen to serve at a later date.

Nutritional Values

Calories 320, Total Fat 3g, Sat Fat 1g, Cholesterol 40mg, Sodium 190mg, Carbohydrates 49g, Dietary Fiber 3g, Sugar 5g, Protein 23g, Calcium 4%, Iron 15%, Vitamin C 8%, Vitamin A 50%

Fennel Soup

2 tablespoons (1 ounce) butter

1 tablespoon olive oil

3 fennel bulbs, trimmed, cored, and thinly sliced

4 cups vegetable broth

Salt and pepper

2 tablespoons grated Parmesan cheese

SERVES 4

1. Melt the butter and olive oil in a large skillet over medium heat. Add the fennel; cook and stir until golden brown, about 10 minutes. Add the broth and simmer until the fennel is tender, about 15 minutes.

2. Working in batches, transfer to a blender or food processor and process until slightly chunky.

3. Return the puréed soup to the pot, season with salt and pepper to taste, and reheat just until warmed through. Divide into bowls, sprinkle each serving with Parmesan, and serve.

Also helpful for: SM, WGP, N

You can garnish this easy soup with toasted fennel seeds or chopped fennel fronds. With the vegetables strained out, this makes a nice alternative to chicken broth for those restricted to a clear liquid diet.

Nutritional Values

Calories 110, Total Fat 6g, Sat Fat 3g, Cholesterol 10mg, Sodium 350mg, Carbohydrates 10g, Dietary Fiber 4g, Sugar 2g, Protein 2g, Calcium 10%, Iron 6%, Vitamin C 20%, Vitamin A 15%

Baked Summer Squash

½ cup fresh bread crumbs

¼ cup grated Parmesan cheese

6 tablespoons (3 ounces) unsalted butter, softened

1 large onion, chopped

3 garlic cloves, minced

8 ounces ground turkey

¼ cup water

3 tablespoons chopped fresh parsley

⅛ teaspoon ground allspice

3 medium summer squashes or zucchini

Salt and pepper

SERVES 6

1. Preheat the oven to 350 degrees. Grease a 9 x 13-inch baking pan and set aside.

2. In a small bowl, mix the bread crumbs, Parmesan, and 3 tablespoons of the butter, melted. Set aside.

2. Heat 3 tablespoons of the butter in a large skillet over medium heat, add the onion and garlic, and cook until golden brown, about 10 minutes. Transfer to a bowl. Add the turkey and water to the empty skillet and cook, stirring, until the water has evaporated and the turkey is cooked through and no longer pink, about 5 minutes. Transfer the turkey to the bowl with the onion and garlic, then add ⅔ of the bread crumb mixture, parsley, and allspice and stir thoroughly to combine.

3. Cut the squashes in half lengthwise and scoop out the center, leaving a ½-inch shell. Place the scooped-out squash in a fine-mesh strainer and let drain for a few minutes, then add to the turkey mixture. Season with salt and pepper to taste.

4. Arrange the squash shells in the prepared pan and divide the filling equally among them. Sprinkle the remaining bread crumb mixture evenly over the stuffed squash. Cover and bake for 15 minutes, then uncover and bake until the topping is crisp and lightly browned, about 15 minutes. Serve.

Also helpful for: WGP, N

Make sure you leave a thick enough shell or the squashes will be too flimsy. Serve with a dollop of plain yogurt if you like.

Nutritional Values

Calories 270, Total Fat 19g, Sat Fat
10g, Cholesterol 65mg, Sodium 190mg,
Carbohydrates 15g, Dietary Fiber 3g, Sugar
5g, Protein 13g, Calcium 15%, Iron 10%,
Vitamin C 50%, Vitamin A 20%

Honey-Roasted Sweet Potatoes

2 pounds red-skinned sweet potatoes, peeled and thinly sliced

¼ cup olive oil

¼ cup honey

¼ cup fresh lemon juice

2 teaspoons ground ginger

½ teaspoon salt

SERVES 6

1. Preheat the oven to 400 degrees. Arrange the sweet potato slices in a 9 x 13-inch baking dish. In a small bowl, whisk together the olive oil, honey, lemon juice, and ginger. Pour the oil mixture over the potatoes and toss to coat. Sprinkle with the salt.

2. Bake until the potatoes are tender, about 1 hour, removing from the oven every 20 minutes to stir. Serve.

Also helpful for: SM. WGP. N

Nutritional Values

Calories 260, Total Fat 9g, Sat Fat 1.5g, Cholesterol 0mg, Sodium 280mg, Carbohydrates 43g, Dietary Fiber 5g, Sugar 17g, Protein 3g, Calcium 4%, Iron 6%, Vitamin C 15%, Vitamin A 430%

Coconut Rice

2 cups long-grain white rice, rinsed

2 cups coconut milk

1 cup water

1 ½ teaspoons ground cinnamon

¼ teaspoon salt

Grated zest of 1 lime

SERVES 8

1. Combine the rice, coconut milk, water, cinnamon, and salt in a medium saucepan. Bring to a boil, lower the heat, cover, and simmer until the rice is tender, about 15 minutes.

2. Remove from the heat, add the lime zest, stir with a fork, cover, and let sit for 10 minutes. Serve.

Also helpful for: WLP, N

Add ground ginger, shredded coconut, or slivered almonds with the lime zest, if desired.

Nutritional Values

Calories 270, Total Fat 12g, Sat Fat 11g, Cholesterol 0mg, Sodium 80mg, Carbohydrates 38g, Dietary Fiber 1g, Sugar 0g, Protein 4g, Calcium 2%, Iron 20%, Vitamin C 6%, Vitamin A 0%

Lemon-Dill Orzo with Chicken

4 cups low-sodium chicken broth

¾ cup water

1 tablespoon unsalted butter

1 ¼ teaspoons kosher salt

¼ teaspoon pepper

1 pound boneless, skinless chicken breasts, trimmed and cut into 1-inch pieces

1 pound orzo

4 ounces feta cheese, crumbled (2 cups)

¼ cup coarsely chopped fresh dill

1 tablespoon fresh lemon juice

1 teaspoon finely grated lemon zest

2 ounces Parmesan cheese, grated (1 cup)

SERVES 10

1. Preheat the oven to 400 degrees. Combine the broth, water, butter, salt, and pepper in a medium saucepan and bring to a boil.

2. Combine the chicken, orzo, feta, dill, lemon juice, and lemon zest in a 9 x 13-inch baking dish. Pour the broth mixture over the orzo and stir to incorporate. Bake until the orzo is tender and the cooking liquid is creamy, about 40 minutes. Sprinkle the Parmesan on top and let stand 5 minutes before serving.

Also helpful for: SM. WLP. N

Make sure you zest the lemon before juicing it.

Nutritional Values

Calories 350, Total Fat 11g, Sat Fat 6g, Cholesterol 60mg, Sodium 760mg, Carbohydrates 35g, Dietary Fiber 2g, Sugar 2g, Protein 24g, Calcium 25%, Iron 10%, Vitamin C 2%, Vitamin A 8%

Chicken and Dumplings

2 tablespoons (1 ounce) unsalted butter

1 tablespoon olive oil

1 russet potato, peeled and diced

2 medium carrots, peeled and diced
or thinly sliced

1 onion, chopped

1 celery rib, chopped

1 teaspoon poultry seasoning

1 bay leaf

Salt and pepper

2 tablespoons all-purpose flour

4 cups low-sodium chicken broth

1 ½ pounds boneless, skinless chicken
breasts, trimmed and cut into 1-inch pieces

1 (8-ounce) box biscuit mix,
such as Jiffy brand

½ cup warm water

¼ cup chopped fresh parsley

1 cup frozen green peas

SERVES 8

1. Heat the butter and oil in a Dutch oven over
   medium-high heat; add the potato, carrots,
   onion, celery, poultry seasoning, bay leaf, and
   salt and pepper to taste and cook for 5 minutes,
   stirring frequently.

2. Add the flour and cook for 2 minutes. Stir in
   the broth and bring to a boil. Add the chicken,
   stir, and simmer until the chicken is no longer
   pink and the vegetables are almost tender,
   about 5 minutes.

3. Meanwhile, combine the biscuit mix with the
   water and parsley. Drop by tablespoons into
   the pot, spacing the dumplings evenly. Cover
   the pot, reduce the heat to medium-low, and
   cook for 8 to 10 minutes.

4. Add the peas, stir, and cook just until the peas
   are heated through. Serve.

Also helpful for: WLP, N

Nutritional Values

Calories 450, Total Fat 21g, Sat Fat
6g, Cholesterol 45mg, Sodium 980mg,
Carbohydrates 47g, Dietary Fiber 3g, Sugar
3g, Protein 18g, Calcium 4%, Iron 15%,
Vitamin C 15%, Vitamin A 60%

Almond Biscotti

2 cups all-purpose flour

2 teaspoons baking powder

⅛ teaspoon salt

½ cup (4 ounces) unsalted butter

1 cup plus 2 tablespoons sugar

3 large eggs

1 teaspoon almond extract

½ cup chopped almonds

2 teaspoons whole milk

MAKES 42 BISCOTTI

1. Preheat the oven to 375 degrees. Line a baking sheet with parchment paper. Whisk together the flour, baking powder, and salt.

2. Using an electric mixer, cream the butter and 1 cup of the sugar. Add the eggs, one at a time, beating well after each addition. Add the almond extract. Stir in the flour mixture, in three additions, then stir in the almonds.

3. Turn the dough out onto a lightly floured surface, divide in half, and roll each half into a log. Place the logs on the prepared baking sheet and press them each into a 12 x 3-inch rectangle. Brush the dough with the milk and sprinkle with the remaining 2 tablespoons sugar. Bake until golden brown and firm to the touch, 20 to 25 minutes.

4. Remove the baking sheet from the oven and reduce the oven temperature to 300 degrees. Using the parchment paper as a handle, slide the rectangles of dough onto a wire rack; let cool for 15 minutes. Working one at a time, place the rectangles of dough on a cutting board and slice diagonally ½ inch thick. Place the slices with a cut side down on the baking sheet. Bake for 10 minutes, then turn the cookies over and bake 10 minutes more. Turn the oven off, open the oven door slightly, and leave the cookies in the oven to cool completely. Store in an airtight container.

Also helpful for: N

Biscotti can be frozen.

Nutritional Values

Calories 80, Total Fat 3.5g, Sat Fat 1.5g, Cholesterol 20mg, Sodium 15mg, Carbohydrates 10g, Dietary Fiber 0g, Sugar 6g, Protein 1g, Calcium 0%, Iron 2%, Vitamin C 0%, Vitamin A 2%

Juice-Tea

1 ½ cups brewed peppermint, ginger, anise, or other herbal tea

1 ½ cups juice, Enlive! juice supplement, or ginger ale

Minced fresh herbs, such as mint (optional)

Honey (optional)

SERVES 3

While tea is brewing, add honey, to taste, if using. Combine the tea and juice in a small pitcher or beverage container (1 quart or larger), add herbs, if using, and refrigerate until needed.

Also helpful for: N

This refreshing beverage may help with nausea between meals, as well as replace any fluids lost from vomiting. Keep some on hand in the refrigerator and serve over ice if you like.

Nutritional Values

Calories 120, Total Fat 0g, Sat Fat 0g, Cholesterol 0mg, Sodium 20mg, Carbohydrates 26g, Dietary Fiber 0g, Sugar 16g, Protein 4g, Calcium 2%, Iron 8%, Vitamin C 20%, Vitamin A 10%

Spiced Cider

4 cups pasteurized apple cider

1 orange, sliced

2 tablespoons honey

1 (1-inch) piece fresh ginger, thinly sliced

1 (3-inch) cinnamon stick

3 whole cloves

SERVES 4

Combine the cider, orange slices, honey, ginger, cinnamon, and cloves in a small saucepan over low heat. Simmer for 8 to 10 minutes, then pour through a fine-mesh strainer into mugs and serve.

Also helpful for: C, N

To make a spiced cider granita, let the cider mixture cool, then strain into an 8- or 9-inch square metal baking pan and place in the freezer until the edges set, about 1 hour. Stir the mixture, return it to the freezer for another hour (until slushy) and stir again. Freeze until solid (at least 3 hours), then, using a fork, scrape the frozen cider to make crystals. Refreeze until needed.

Nutritional Values

Calories 170, Total Fat 0g, Sat Fat 0g, Cholesterol 0mg, Sodium 25mg, Carbohydrates 43g, Dietary Fiber 1g, Sugar 37g, Protein 0g, Calcium 2%, Iron 0%, Vitamin C 30%, Vitamin A 2%

CELEBRATIONS

As difficult as cancer treatment is, it is not all hard times and side effects. In among the drudgery of doctors' visits, lab tests, scans, and all kinds of medical interventions, there are frequent episodes that lighten the burden. A good blood value, improvement in the MRI, resolution of symptoms—any welcome news can be a reason to celebrate. Even more significant for many people is the end of cancer treatment, which can feel like a sort of graduation. Marking the transition from cancer patient to survivor, the day that you finish chemotherapy, radiation, and surgery, is truly time to celebrate.

This chapter includes recipes that are a little more special—dishes around which a celebration can be based. It also contains recipes for cocktails to enjoy on special occasions.

Drinking Alcohol during Cancer Treatment

Patients often ask about drinking alcohol during and after cancer treatments. Here are some recommendations:

• Moderation is key. The American Cancer Society recommends that men limit their intake to no more than two drinks per day and women, one.

• Alcohol should be avoided at certain times during cancer treatment. For example, alcohol can irritate mouth sores and also contribute to dehydration. It should be avoided immediately after chemotherapy when the focus should be on increasing fluid intake. If you have liver disease of any kind, ask your doctor whether a little alcohol would be safe.

• For people who have completed cancer treatment, the effects of alcohol on cancer recurrence risk are largely unknown. It's important to discuss this with your doctor.

• Never drink and drive. Also, be aware that any mental effects of alcohol will be magnified if you are on painkillers.

Lobster Pot Pie

½ cup (4 ounces) unsalted butter

1 ½ cups chopped onions

1 cup chopped fennel

½ cup all-purpose flour

1 ½ cups low-sodium chicken broth

1 cup fish stock or clam juice

¼ cup anise liqueur, such as Sambuca

1 teaspoon kosher salt

1 teaspoon pepper

1 cup diced white potato

1 pound cooked fresh lobster meat, cut into pieces

1 ½ cups frozen peas, thawed

¾ cup frozen pearl onions, thawed

½ cup minced fresh parsley

5 tablespoons heavy cream

4 sheets phyllo dough

1 large egg, lightly beaten

SERVES 4

1. Preheat the oven to 375 degrees. Melt the butter in a large saucepan over medium heat, add the chopped onions and fennel, and cook, stirring, until the vegetables are translucent, about 10 minutes. Add the flour and cook, stirring, for 3 minutes. Slowly add the chicken broth, fish stock, liqueur, salt, and pepper and whisk to combine. Add the potatoes and cook for 10 minutes. Add the lobster, peas, pearl onions, parsley, and cream to the sauce and mix well.

2. Transfer the mixture to a 9 x 13-inch baking dish. Cover with the phyllo dough, folding the dough to fit the pan. Brush the beaten egg over the dough. Bake until the filling is bubbling and the crust is golden brown, about 20 minutes. Serve.

Nutritional Values

Calories 680, Total Fat 34g, Sat Fat 20g, Cholesterol 215mg, Sodium 1240mg, Carbohydrates 53g, Dietary Fiber 7g, Sugar 10g, Protein 35g, Calcium 20%, Iron 25%, Vitamin C 60%, Vitamin A 60%

Strawberry Angel Food Cake

12 large egg whites

1 ¼ cups confectioners' sugar

1 cup all-purpose flour

1 ½ teaspoons vanilla extract

1 ½ teaspoons cream of tartar

¼ teaspoon salt

1 cup granulated sugar

1 (7-ounce) can prepared whipped cream

2 cups sliced strawberries, plus 5 whole strawberries for garnish

SERVES 14

1. Preheat the oven to 350 degrees. Measure the egg whites in a liquid measuring cup; you should have 1 ½ cups (reserve any extra for another use). Transfer to a mixing bowl and let stand at room temperature for 30 minutes. Sift the confectioners' sugar and flour together three times; set aside.

2. Add the vanilla, cream of tartar, and salt to the egg whites; beat with an electric mixer on high speed. Gradually add the granulated sugar, beating until the sugar is dissolved and stiff peaks form. Fold in the flour mixture, ¼ cup at a time.

3. Gently spoon the batter into an ungreased 10-inch tube pan. Cut through the batter with a knife to remove air pockets. Bake until the cake springs back when lightly touched, 40 to 45 minutes. Immediately invert the pan; let cool completely, about 2 hours.

4. Remove the cake from the pan and, using a serrated knife, slice the cake in half horizontally. Place the bottom layer cut side up on a cake platter and spread a thin layer of the whipped cream evenly over the cut surface. Layer half the sliced strawberries over the cream, then spread more cream over the berries. Place the top cake layer, cut side down, on the filling and layer the remaining cream and sliced berries in the same manner. Top with the whole strawberries. Serve, or refrigerate until needed.

Nutritional Values

Calories 200, Total Fat 3g, Sat Fat 2g, Cholesterol 15mg, Sodium 90mg, Carbohydrates 37g, Dietary Fiber 1g, Sugar 28g, Protein 4g, Calcium 0%, Iron 4%, Vitamin C 25%, Vitamin A 0%

Chocolate Cupcakes

2 ⅔ cups all-purpose flour

1 ¼ cups plus 2 tablespoons unsweetened cocoa powder

2 teaspoons baking powder

1 teaspoon baking soda

1 teaspoon salt

1 cup sour cream

1 teaspoon vanilla extract

1 teaspoon almond extract

1 cup (8 ounces) unsalted butter, softened

2 cups sugar

2 large eggs

1 ¼ cups strong brewed coffee, cooled

MAKES 12 CUPCAKES

1. Preheat the oven to 350 degrees. Line a 12-cup muffin tin with paper liners.

2. In a large bowl, sift together the flour, cocoa powder, baking powder, baking soda, and salt. Combine the sour cream, vanilla, and almond extract in a separate bowl.

3. Using an electric mixer, beat the butter and sugar on medium speed until smooth. Reduce the speed to low and add the eggs, one at a time, scraping the bowl after each addition. Add the flour in three additions alternately with the sour cream mixture in two additions, scraping down the bowl after each addition. Gradually pour in the coffee. Scrape down the bowl and beat thoroughly combined.

4. Divide the batter evenly among the muffin cups. Bake the cupcakes until a toothpick inserted in the center comes out clean, 20 to 25 minutes. Let the cupcakes cool for 5 minutes in the tin, then turn out onto a wire rack to cool completely. Serve plain or frost with your favorite frosting.

You can use Classic Chocolate Buttercream (page 176) or Vanilla Buttercream (page 177) to frost these cupcakes.

Nutritional Values

Calories 460, Total Fat 21g, Sat Fat 12g, Cholesterol 85mg, Sodium 220mg, Carbohydrates 62g, Dietary Fiber 3g, Sugar 35g, Protein 7g, Calcium 4%, Iron 15%, Vitamin C 0%, Vitamin A 15%

White Celebration Cake

4 ½ cups cake flour (not self-rising)

2 tablespoons baking powder

1 ½ teaspoons salt

1 ½ cups whole milk

9 large egg whites, lightly beaten

1 tablespoon vanilla extract

½ teaspoon almond extract

1 cup (8 ounces) unsalted butter, room temperature

2 ¼ cups sugar

SERVES 14

1. Preheat the oven to 350 degrees. Grease and flour three 9-inch round cake pans; set aside. Sift together the flour, baking powder, and salt. Whisk the milk, egg whites, vanilla, and almond extract together in a bowl.

2. Using an electric mixer, beat the butter for 30 seconds. Gradually add the sugar and continue beating until light and fluffy, about 2 minutes. Add the flour in three additions alternately with the milk mixture two additions, scraping down the bowl after each addition. Divide the batter equally among the prepared pans and smooth the surface with a rubber spatula. Bake until the top of each cake springs back when lightly pressed and a cake tester comes out clean, 25 to 30 minutes.

3. Let the cakes cool in the pans on wire racks for 5 minutes, then run a knife around the edge of the pans and invert the cakes directly onto the racks. Re-invert and let cool completely. Frost as desired.

You can use Classic Chocolate Buttercream (page 176) or Vanilla Buttercream (page 177) to frost this cake.

Nutritional Values

Calories 470, Total Fat 17g, Sat Fat 10g, Cholesterol 155mg, Sodium 540mg, Carbohydrates 70g, Dietary Fiber 1g, Sugar 35g, Protein 9g, Calcium 10%, Iron 20%, Vitamin C 0%, Vitamin A 10%

Classic Chocolate Buttercream

6 large egg whites, room temperature

1 cup sugar

¼ cup water

1 pound unsalted butter, cut into
32 pieces, softened

6 ounces bittersweet chocolate, melted
and cooled to room temperature

**MAKES ENOUGH TO FROST ONE 9-INCH
LAYER CAKE.**

1. With an electric mixer, beat the egg whites to
   soft peaks. Meanwhile, combine the sugar and
   water in a small saucepan and cook, stirring to
   dissolve the sugar, over high heat until the syrup
   reaches 238 degrees (the soft ball stage).

2. Immediately, with the mixer on low speed,
   slowly add the hot syrup to the whites, being
   careful not to let the syrup hit the beaters. Once
   all the syrup is incorporated, return the speed to
   high and beat until the whites have cooled.

3. Reduce the speed to low and add the butter
   1 tablespoon at a time until completely
   incorporated, then increase the speed to high
   and beat to a glossy, fluffy consistency. Using
   a rubber spatula, fold in the melted chocolate
   until smooth.

Nutritional Values

Calories 360, Total Fat 32g, Sat Fat
19g, Cholesterol 70mg, Sodium 25mg,
Carbohydrates 21g, Dietary Fiber 1g, Sugar
19g, Protein 3g, Calcium 0%, Iron 2%,
Vitamin C 0%, Vitamin A 15%

Vanilla Buttercream

½ cup solid vegetable shortening

½ cup (4 ounces) unsalted butter, softened

1 teaspoon vanilla extract

4 cups (1 pound) confectioners' sugar, sifted

2–4 tablespoons whole milk

MAKES ENOUGH TO FROST ONE 9-INCH LAYER CAKE

1. Beat the shortening and butter with an electric mixer until light and fluffy. Add the vanilla and beat to incorporate. Gradually add the sugar, 1 cup at a time, beating on medium speed and scraping the sides and bottom of the bowl as necessary.

2. Add 2 tablespoons of the milk and beat at medium speed until light and fluffy. Add the remaining milk as needed for a smooth and spreadable consistency. Keep the frosting covered with a damp cloth until ready to use.

This icing can be stored, refrigerated in an airtight container, for 2 weeks. Rewhip before using.

Nutritional Values

Calories 260, Total Fat 13g, Sat Fat 6g, Cholesterol 15mg, Sodium 0mg, Carbohydrates 34g, Dietary Fiber 0g, Sugar 34g, Protein 0g, Calcium 0%, Iron 0%, Vitamin C 0%, Vitamin A 4%

Hot Fudge Sauce

7 tablespoons (3 ½ ounces) unsalted butter

2 ½ ounces unsweetened chocolate

1 cup plus 1 tablespoon Dutch cocoa

1 cup plus 2 tablespoons superfine sugar

5 tablespoons whole milk

5 tablespoons heavy cream

SERVES 14

Melt the butter and chocolate in a medium saucepan over low heat, stirring frequently. Slowly add the cocoa and sugar, stirring to dissolve. Add the milk and cream and continue to cook, stirring, until the cocoa and sugar are completely dissolved and the mixture is smooth. Use immediately or let cool and store in the refrigerator until needed. Reheat gently before serving.

Use the best chocolate and cocoa you can find.

If you can't find superfine sugar, process an equal amount of granulated sugar in a food processor for 30 seconds. Store in the refrigerator for up to 1 year.

Nutritional Values

Calories 190, Total Fat 11g, Sat Fat 7g, Cholesterol 25mg, Sodium 5mg, Carbohydrates 22g, Dietary Fiber 1g, Sugar 17g, Protein 2g, Calcium 2%, Iron 15%, Vitamin C 0%, Vitamin A 6%

Cool Energy Spritzer

½ cup orange sports drink
(such as Gatorade)

½ cup orange juice

½ cup lemon-lime soda

¼ cup vodka

1 splash cranberry juice

Ice cubes

1 lime wedge

orange slice

SERVES 1

Mix the sports drink, orange juice, soda,
vodka, and cranberry juice in a large liquid
measuring cup. Fill a glass with ice cubes,
pour the spritzer over the ice, and squeeze
the lime wedge into the glass. Add orange
slice and serve.

Nutritional Values

Calories 170, Total Fat 0g, Sat Fat 0g,
Cholesterol 0mg, Sodium 20mg,
Carbohydrates 10g, Dietary Fiber 0g, Sugar
8g, Protein 0g, Calcium 0%, Iron 0%,
Vitamin C 15%, Vitamin A 0%

Cordless Screwdriver

1 tablespoon sugar

1 orange slice

¼ cup lemon or citron-flavored vodka

2 tablespoons triple sec

1 splash fresh lime juice

1 splash orange juice

3–5 ice cubes

SERVES 1

1. Pour the sugar into a saucer or small, shallow dish. Rub the edge of a martini glass with the orange slice (reserve the slice for garnish), then dip into the sugar to coat the rim. Place the glass in the refrigerator or freezer to chill.

2. Combine the vodka, triple sec, lime juice, orange juice, and ice cubes in a shaker and shake will. Strain the mixture into the chilled glass, garnish with the reserved orange slice, and serve immediately.

Nutritional Values

Calories 150, Total Fat 0g, Sat Fat 0g, Cholesterol 0mg, Sodium 5mg, Carbohydrates 18g, Dietary Fiber 0g, Sugar 17g, Protein 0g, Calcium 0%, Iron 0%, Vitamin C 4%, Vitamin A 0%

Great Grape Crush

4 cups seedless red grapes, 4 set aside as garnish

2 tablespoons fresh lemon juice

2 tablespoons honey

2 cups seltzer

¾ cup vodka

Crushed ice

Lemon wedge, for garnish

SERVES 4

1. Place the grapes in a blender and process until smooth. Set a fine-mesh strainer over a medium bowl. Pour the purée through the strainer, pressing on the solids to extract all the juice. Add the lemon juice and honey to the grape juice and stir until the honey is dissolved.

2. Add the seltzer and vodka to the grape juice mixture and stir to blend. Fill four glasses with crushed ice and divide the grape-seltzer mixture among the glasses. Garnish with the whole grapes and lemon wedge and serve.

Nutritional Values

Calories 190, Total Fat 0g, Sat Fat 0g, Cholesterol 0mg, Sodium 0mg, Carbohydrates 25g, Dietary Fiber 1g, Sugar 23g, Protein 1g, Calcium 2%, Iron 2%, Vitamin C 10%, Vitamin A 2%

Green with Envy Daiquiris

2 (12-ounce) cans frozen limeade concentrate, thawed

2 cups lemon-lime sports drink (such as Gatorade), chilled

1 cup light rum

2 (12-ounce) cans lemon-lime soda, chilled

1 lime, sliced

SERVES 9

1. Mix the limeade concentrate, lemon-lime sports drink, and rum in a large pitcher. Refrigerate until needed.

2. Add the soda, pour into ice-filled glasses, garnish with lime slices, and serve.

Nutritional Values

Calories 110, Total Fat 0g, Sat Fat 0g, Cholesterol 0mg, Sodium 35mg, Carbohydrates 14g, Dietary Fiber 0g, Sugar 12g, Protein 0g, Calcium 0%, Iron 0%, Vitamin C 4%, Vitamin A 0%

Sunrise Martini

1 tablespoon sugar

2 tablespoons fresh lemon juice

¼ cup gin

2 tablespoons fresh grapefruit juice

1 large egg white

1 tablespoon triple sec

3–5 ice cubes

Mint sprig, for garnish

SERVES 1

1. Pour the sugar into a saucer or small, shallow dish. Rub the edge of a martini glass with the lemon juice, then dip into the sugar to coat the rim. Place the glass in the refrigerator or freezer to chill.

2. Combine the gin, grapefruit juice, egg white, triple sec, and ice cubes in a shaker and shake well. Strain the mixture into the chilled glass, add mint sprig for garnish, and serve immediately.

PLEASE NOTE: This beverage contains a raw egg and should not be consumed by neutropenic patients.

Nutritional Values

Calories 180, Total Fat 0g, Sat Fat 0g, Cholesterol 0mg, Sodium 65mg, Carbohydrates 25g, Dietary Fiber 0g, Sugar 23g, Protein 4g, Calcium 0%, Iron 0%, Vitamin C 15%, Vitamin A 0%

Summer Sangria

1 (750-milliliter) bottle white wine

⅔ cup sugar

3 oranges, sliced, or 1 cup fresh orange juice

1 lemon, sliced

1 lime, sliced

2 cups ginger ale

Ice cubes

SERVES 12

Pour the wine into a large pitcher, add the sugar, and stir to dissolve. Squeeze the fruit into the wine, then drop in the slices. Refrigerate until needed. Just before serving, add the ginger ale. Serve over ice.

Make sure to thoroughly wash and dry the oranges and lemons before you slice them. For extra fiber and flavor, add sliced peaches, pears, apples and/or fresh berries.

Nutritional Values

Calories 50, Total Fat 0g, Sat Fat 0g, Cholesterol 0mg, Sodium 0mg, Carbohydrates 11g, Dietary Fiber 0g, Sugar 10g, Protein 0g, Calcium 0%, Iron 0%, Vitamin C 10%, Vitamin A 0%

LiMango Frappes

1 mango, peeled, pitted, and cut into chunks

¾ cup fresh orange juice

¼ cup fresh lime juice

1 ¼ cups club soda

2 ice cubes

SERVES 3

Place the mango in a blender and process until smooth. Add the orange juice and lime juice and process. Add the club soda and ice cubes and pulse the blender until the cubes are crushed and the ingredients are blended. Serve.

Nutritional Values

Calories 100, Total Fat 0g, Sat Fat 0g, Cholesterol 0mg, Sodium 25mg, Carbohydrates 25g, Dietary Fiber 2g, Sugar 21g, Protein 1g, Calcium 2%, Iron 2%, Vitamin C 110%

Sporting Smoothies

2 cups ice cubes

2 scoops vanilla ice cream

2 cups grape-flavored sports drink

Place all the ingredients in a blender and process until smooth. Serve.

Nutritional Values

Calories 210, Total Fat 10g, Sat Fat 6g, Cholesterol 60mg, Sodium 140mg, Carbohydrates 28g, Dietary Fiber 0g, Sugar 28g, Protein 3g, Calcium 10%, Iron 0%, Vitamin C 0%, Vitamin A 6%

Acknowledgments

Like any major project, this cancer cookbook is the result of countless hours of developing, testing, tasting, editing, modifying and photographing hundreds of recipes. Lahey Clinic would like to thank the following people who had the vision and drive to create something very unique and valuable. Without everyone's hard work, this project could not have been possible.

Corrine Zarwan, MD; Keith Stuart, MD; F. W. Nugent, MD; Elizabeth Collins, MD; Joan Alosso; Christine Benecchi; Gina Bolognese; Joyce Byron; Erika Clapp; Linda Clay; Margie Coloian; Elizabeth Fayram; Nellie Fine, RN; Holly Guarino; Brenda Hill, RN; Kathryn Mulholland; Kathleen Nardini; Colleen O'Brien; Jeffrey O'Brien; Michelle O'Brien; Pamela Reznick, CSW; Stephanie Saia; Nancy Stuart; Elizabeth Rose Underhill; Jo Underhill, RN; Holly Williams, RD

Special thanks to the following people who contributed their special talents to ensure our success.

Ann Collette, Agent, Rees Literary Agency
Roberta L. Dowling, CCP, Cambridge School of Culinary Arts, and the following staff members of the Cambridge School of Culinary Arts:

Julie Burba, Cesare Casadei, Mark Farone, John Hannon, Eliana Hussain, Lori O'Neil, Michael Pavloski, Anne Quinn, Brian Seymour, Stephan Viau, Theodore Villa

Robert Mailloux and Scott Morton, LaPlume Printing

Leise Jones Smyrl, Leise Jones Photography

Most of all, we would like to thank the patients and families from the Sophia Gordon Cancer Center at Lahey Clinic for inspiring us to write this book.

INDEX